MW01166680

letter to the

Ephesians

Henry Vander Kam

Reformed Fellowship, Inc.
3363 Hickory Ridge Ct. SW
Grandville, MI 49418

For information:
Reformed Fellowship, Inc.
3363 Hickory Ridge Ct. SW
Grandville, MI 49418
Phone: 616.532.8510
Web: reformedfellowship.net
Email: sales@reformedfellowship.net

Book design by Jeff Steenholdt

ISBN 0-9653981-8-8

Contents

Our Glorious Redemption

Ephesians 1:1-14

A Letter About Christ's Church

Paul wrote this beautiful epistle while he was a prisoner in Rome. He had been working in Ephesus for some time and apparently a sizeable church was found in this city at the time this letter was written. In this letter he speaks of the Church of Jesus Christ and the unity of the Church.

There is some debate about the address of this epistle. The most ancient manuscripts do not contain the words "at Ephesus" in the first verse. However, most of the manuscripts do contain these words and it is quite certain that this epistle was addressed to Ephesus and the surrounding territory.

Paul introduces himself as the writer and immediately adds that he is an Apostle of Christ Jesus through the will of God. He comes with the word of God and of Christ. His word is, therefore, not to be considered to be only the word of a man, but he comes with divine authority. His word is to be accepted as the word of God, a word on which the hearers or readers may rely for their eternal salvation. He writes to those who have been separated by God for a definite purpose and believe on His name. Upon these he pronounces the blessing of God. His unmerited favor is given them (grace), and the inner peace which only God can give, is extended to them. This is the *Church*, the body of Christ, which has been set aside for His service and whose members enjoy a peace which no other people have ever received.

Except for the salutation there are no introductory

remarks. He at once begins with the body of this letter. He is ecstatic! His consuming passion for the gospel is perhaps more clearly stated here than in any of his writings. He heaps the many thoughts which come to his mind on top of each other. Here is a man who not only preaches the gospel but has himself become totally captivated by it. The verses three to fourteen form one sentence! He is not able to make a simple statement concerning the gospel of Christ. As soon as he has said the one thing, many other thoughts crowd his mind. The redemption of God's people is not merely a fact — it is such a glorious fact that human language is not sufficient to express it.

Thanks for Every Spiritual Blessing

He begins with his adoration of God. God, the Father of our Lord Jesus Christ, is the author of our salvation. No one will ever be able to give sufficient thanks to Him. Let men worship Him day and night as long as they live. He is the One who has sent His Son and He sent Him as an evidence of the great love wherewith He loved us. He is the One who has given us all the spiritual blessings. These are far more than material gifts. These are the blessings on which we live now and into eternity. These blessings are, therefore, heavenly in origin. All these blessings are ours "*in* Christ." How often he uses that expression, especially in this epistle. By it he refers to our union with Christ. There are no blessings outside of Christ. Believing on Him means to be united to Him. So he will also speak of the church in the following chapters. That church has no existence by itself. Its union with Christ determines the nature and function of that church. Anyone who would know the meaning of the term *church* must study Ephesians.

Based on God's Eternal Choice

To realize the nature of the spiritual blessings which we

have in Him, the author now shows us the foundation on which these blessings rest. He chose us in Him before the foundation of the world. This is election. This is not an abstract term for him, but it is throbbing with life. He chose us! This is not something to be debated as to reason and method etc., but must be completely accepted as an established fact. Nor does election bring to mind an arbitrary will at work, but the gracious work of our heavenly Father! This choosing was done apart from us, i.e., we had nothing to do with it. He chose us in Him, in Christ, before the foundation of the world. His people were given to the Christ. In union with Him they have been chosen. He chose long before our lives began on this earth. He did not choose us because of anything in us or because He knew we would believe, no, He chose us *so that* we would be holy and without blemish before Him in love.

Adopted Sons of God

What a glorious thing that we have been chosen unto salvation! But, there is more. Our wealth in Him cannot be measured. He also foreordained us (or elected us) unto adoption as sons! Being saved has not only a negative aspect, that we will not suffer eternal punishment, it has many glorious positive aspects. We are now sons of God by adoption. This is the clearest term the Bible is able to use to describe our relation to Him, but it is not wholly adequate. Scripture also speaks of us as "born of God" — adopted, yet born of Him. Peter even speaks of the divine nature being imparted to us. However, we understand the Apostle's terminology. As adopted sons we have all the rights and privileges of sonship. This adoption occurred through Christ. This was His good pleasure. God delights in the salvation of His people.

Salvation

The election of God had as its purpose to save His people. This salvation was accomplished. However, the ultimate purpose of His election was "the praise of the glory of His grace." His goodness, His love, His grace is magnified by the election of His people. They may never lose sight of it. His goodness, love and grace is seen everywhere but most clearly in the salvation of His own. He has bestowed all of this on us freely in Jesus Christ. His grace is so great — and He has made us the recipients of it! We have indeed tasted that God is good.

Bought by Christ

As the multitude of thoughts crowd in upon each other as he is describing the glorious salvation which is ours, there is a slight change of emphasis found in verse 7. No, the shift in thought is too small to warrant a new paragraph, but he now emphasizes the work done by Christ in our redemption. Before this he had emphasized the Father's work in choosing us to salvation. Now he speaks of the fact that this redemption has been wrought through the blood of Christ. It is a *redemption*, i.e., a ransom has been paid. Our redemption has been *bought*! The Old Testament already spoke of the ransom which would have to be paid and Jesus spoke of the fact that He had come to give His life as a ransom for many. Silver and gold did not suffice as a ransom. The required payment was enormous — nothing less than the *blood* of the Son of God. But, have no fear, His payment was sufficient. Our trespasses were thereby forgiven! We were purchased unto Himself and no one else had any claim on us from that day on. By that payment He revealed the riches of His grace. And this grace is so great and so rich that it has not only purchased our redemption but it filled His people so that they receive all wisdom and prudence. He has not impoverished Himself when He paid the price of our sin. His riches know no bounds. There was plenty left so that He gave His gifts to His people. Their redemption is not only negative, i.e., that they were freed from something, no, its positive side is so beautiful — He has enriched them so that they now have all things. He made these riches to abound to us. He gave them the wisdom — the proper use of knowledge — and the insight into the wonders of salvation.

A Mystery Revealed

This wisdom and insight are so necessary because He has now made known unto us the mystery of His will. Paul uses this term frequently in his letters. He does not mean something mysterious, but, rather, a making known those things which had not been revealed in former ages. The people to whom he is writing have received a far clearer revelation than former ages had received. These revealed things they must now understand and for that purpose He has given them an abundance of wisdom and insight. In the new revelation of the fullness of redemption He has made known His good pleasure. He rejoices in making known to His people the beauty of their salvation. His purposes now become clear. The Old Testament saints may have wondered at His purposes time and again. The saints of the New Testament times will have a clearer view.

With the coming of Jesus Christ into this world and the work which He has done for our redemption, the purposes of God are realized. This coming of our Lord has brought the dispensation of the fullness of the times. The day of shadows is past. The mystery is now revealed. It is a wholly new and different age. All things are summed up in Christ. He is the One who draws all things together in the whole universe. So many things seemed to be separated before. Men were not able to understand that everything had a purpose. Christ is the One in Whom all things come together. All things are summed up in Him, that is, He is the Head of all things. The world which had fallen into sin and thereby ruined the orderliness originally found in it is restored in Christ. The Christ is of far greater significance for the world than the bringer of redemption in the narrow sense.

God's Heirs in Christ

Christ has been made Head over all things for the benefit of the church and therefore the Apostle, together with other believers, can rejoice in the fact that "we were made a heritage." The recipients of His redemption are also the heirs of all the other benefits found in Christ. God includes all the things which have happened in the past, are happening today and what will happen in the future in His all-embracing plan. He not only makes His plans, He also carries them out. Nothing can foil His plans. Nothing can separate us from the love of God which is in Christ Jesus our Lord. This gives stability and certainty to the lives of believers. We were in that plan of God and He does everything according to the counsel of His will. He has a glorious purpose in mind: that we should be unto the praise of His glory. Here he refers to the purpose of all things as they were intended from the beginning of creation. He created all things to bring praise and glory to His name. This purpose seemed to be thwarted by the entrance of sin into the world, but all things are renewed with the coming of Christ. He reversed the disorder which sin had brought into the world. It has cost a huge price, but God's original purposes are realized! Those who fall heir to these benefits wrought by Christ have had their hope centered in Christ even before all things have been brought to their conclusion. Certainly, their faith is genuine, but all things have not yet been accomplished. Much more is still to come.

Heirs by Faith in the Gospel

He has spoken of the fact that he, together with the believers to whom he is writing, are the heirs of all the blessings wrought by Jesus Christ. How can they know that they truly are such heirs? They had believed the word! That word is the truth! This is said because there were many false 'gospels' at that time as well as in our day. This word of truth was the gospel of their salvation! It is only through belief in the word of truth that salvation will be obtained. You were then sealed with the Holy Spirit of promise, he says. This Spirit had been promised and all promises are realized in Him. The Spirit had authenticated the word which they had believed. In fact, their believing was already His work. The Spirit testifies within them to the truth of the gospel of salvation. The Spirit testifies of Christ. He gives assurances as well as the knowledge of the truth. He wrote the word — he is its best commentator.

The Holy Spirit — A Down-Payment

At the conclusion of this section he calls the Holy Spirit "an earnest of our inheritance." The Spirit is the first installment of our inheritance. The first payment has been made and this is the assurance that the whole inheritance will become ours. We must remember: we are still battling sin, the second coming of our Savior must still come and the bliss of heaven still awaits us. But, the full salvation will come because we have already received the down payment! His promises shall surely come to pass. His purposes shall be realized. He will fully redeem His own possession. This is typically Pauline language. It is also the language of the first question and answer of the Heidelberg Catechism. God made us. He bought us. We belong to Him.

Paul began this section with a doxology and ends it with the words "unto the praise of his glory." He is straining human language to reveal his thanks for what God has done for him through Jesus Christ in the Holy Spirit. Salvation is so beautiful! We owe all to Another. How can men take it lightly!

Questions for discussion:
1. What is Paul's view of his office?
2. Is election of practical benefit for the believer? Is Christian doctrine always practical?
3. How much is involved in our adoption to be children of God?
4. What does it mean that He has summed up all things in Christ?
5. What does the phrase "in Christ" mean?
6. What does our inheritance include?
7. Can people be saved apart from believing the word?

Lesson 2

The Wealth of Believers

Ephesians 1:15-23

Paul has finally come to the end of the long sentence contained in the previous eleven verses in which he has extolled the salvation revealed by the Triune God. He has stressed the work of Father, Son and Holy Spirit. All these works must be seen by the people of God to appreciate the fullness and the beauty of the salvation which has been revealed.

Thanks for the Church

Paul had worked in this church at Ephesus for some time — but that was about four years ago. He worked diligently here and his labors were also crowned with success. Many had come to the faith in this important city. Its church is the first of the churches mentioned by John in the book of Revelation. When John speaks of this church in Revelation 2, it had lost its first love. At the time in which Paul is writing to this people that love is still very much in evidence. Therefore he rejoices in the news he has heard from this church while he himself is in prison. Their faith in Jesus Christ is evident to everyone. They also live their faith because they show their love to all the saints. (The great danger which this church faces some years later when they have lost that first love is that their faith has then died.) Faith shows itself in love and by means of the true love one is able to deduce that the true faith is present. The Apostle rejoices in the good report he hears and that he is thus able to see the continuing work of the Spirit of God in them.

How often this Apostle mentions the fact that he gives

thanks for the faith of the people he is addressing. This is genuine. When he looks back to the time when he came to Ephesus and compares it with the present time, there is indeed reason to rejoice and give thanks. It is true, Apollos had worked there, but his view of the gospel needed correction. When Paul arrived in this city some of the people admitted that they did not even know that Pentecost had come and that they had been baptized with the baptism of John. Paul had a great deal of work to do here and he was given two years to do it. Ah, how that work had been blessed! He is in prison now but he has time for prayer and does not forget this church.

Prayer for the Church

What does he pray for? No doubt he prays that the church may fare well and that it may be kept in the truth. This would be the natural prayer of this former pastor for this church. But, he tells us specifically what he prays for concerning this church. He makes it very clear to them to Whom he prays. He prays to the God of our Lord Jesus Christ, the Father of glory. Strange isn't it that he should speak in this way? Why doesn't he say: I pray to God for you? Remember how he has emphasized the attributes of God in the verses 3-14. Every part of that revelation is important, and must also be recognized in the prayer life of His people. His people don't just pray! Some have the idea today that God is standing at their elbow and is ready to do the bidding of the one who "prays" as though He is his servant. No, we come to the God of Jesus Christ. He is the Father of glory. Let there be awe in prayer!

Prayer for Vision

What does he pray for them? The content of his prayer sounds rather strange to us. He prays that God may give them His Holy Spirit so that they may have wisdom and revelation in the knowledge of Him. Certainly, only the Spirit of God will be able to give such wisdom in the revelation He has given of Himself so that they may come to an understanding of Him. They do have this knowledge, but he wishes them to increase in this knowledge. All their knowledge of Him must come by revelation. Let them then work diligently with the revelation they have received and may the Spirit of God illumine their minds.

Paul continues his train of thought in verse 18, but again uses some strange language to make clear what he has in mind. He prays that "the eyes of their hearts may be enlightened." That is the only way they will come to the proper knowledge of God and of His gifts. By the term "heart" the Scriptures refer to the core of man's being. Now, to see with the heart and not only with the physical eye is the concern of the Apostle in this verse. The "eye" of the natural man's heart is blind. He cannot see anything but that which is observable by the physical eye. Believers are of a different nature. That which eye has not seen is nevertheless believed! They do not only live by that which the natural eye is able to see. The Spirit of God has given them a vision which others are not able to perceive. Only if the eye of the heart is enlightened will they be able to realize the hope of His calling. What does the natural man know about an inner call? Only if the heart's eye is enlightened will he be able to understand the riches of the glory of God's inheritance in the saints. Together with all other believers they have this assured knowledge. This is the essence of faith! You can tell someone about the hope you have, but if his heart's eye is not enlightened you are speaking in riddles in his estimation. The believer's life is so much richer than he is able to imagine.

God's Power

The believer is dependent on the enlightenment of the

heart's eye for all the spiritual benefits he receives. By that enlightenment the hope is real, the faith is placed on a solid foundation and the believer recognizes the tremendous power of God which has been exerted in order that we might obtain salvation. The power of God is usually spoken of in regard to the mighty works we see in nature. This is Biblical too. The book of Job speaks of the powers of God as they are shown in the mighty storms which rage over the earth and in His creation of powerful creatures, and His power displayed in the orderliness of all things. However, when we deal with the subject of salvation we usually emphasize the love and grace of God. This too is Biblical. Time and again the Bible speaks of the great love He had for those whom He had chosen and that their very choice revealed His grace. But, the power of God which has been revealed in the salvation of His people may not be overlooked. His power also makes our hope sure — no one shall snatch us out of His powerful grasp.

This power of God is shown especially in the fact that He raised Christ from the dead and caused Him to be seated at the place of power in the heavens. We may never become so accustomed to the knowledge of the resurrection of Christ that we fail to see the marvel of it. It seemed as though death would reign and have the preeminence as long as the world would stand. However, God reached down with His almighty power and raised Him from the dead, thereby conquering death for all those whose heart's eye has been enlightened. It is also well for us to note how often Paul speaks of the exalted and ruling Christ of the present time. The church has not grasped this fact fully even to the present day! Several churches have to meet together on Ascension Day in order to make it worthwhile to have a service! What a shame! Paul becomes ecstatic when he thinks of Christ's present position because that is the guarantee of his present safety and future goal!

Christ's Ascendant Power

Christ, he says, is ascended far above all the powers you may imagine. No one can compare with Him. He is not speaking now of human rule but the rule of angels too. Human rule is often praised and its might revered. But, human rule and might is not found in the heavenly places nor is it named in both this world and the next. We know from the Scriptures that the angels are powerful and that their power and rule exceeds that of men so far that it cannot be measured. An angel stands on the threshing floor in David's time and slays thousands in Israel and it seems as though nothing can stop him. Angels will have a prominent place at the time of the return of our Lord. But, Christ stands far above them all! God gave Him authority over all things. By virtue of the fact that He rose from the dead He says: All authority is mine both in heaven and on earth! No, He does not stand as a beggar before men to ask whether or not they will have Him! All authority is His and He exercises it! This makes the lot of the believer glorious. There is absolutely nothing which can prevent his hope from being realized. Surely, we must see Christ's love and grace displayed, but we have a very warped view of salvation if that is our only basis of hope. Paul emphasizes both the aspects of love and power and we must do the same, or we impoverish ourselves.

Sovereign Head

Christ has all things made subject to Him and He has also been made the Head over all things. This is the complete picture of His absolute sovereignty. Now the Apostle tells us what is the immediate purpose of this sovereignty. He has been given all this authority for the benefit of the *church*. As I said before, Ephesians stresses the nature and importance of the church as virtually no other book of the New Testament. Later (5:25-33) he will speak of the Head-body symbolism. Here he speaks of the fact that Christ has received all rule for the benefit of the church. No one can, therefore, understand the history of the world apart from the history of the church. The church stands at the center of all things. That church is His body. This is already preparatory to the things Paul is going to say about the church in chapter 5. Much, is made of personal salvation today—know Jesus as your personal Savior! Of course, this cannot be denied. But, the nature and importance of the church is minimized in many circles today! "You will not be asked to which church you belonged on earth!" Many seem to know that this question will not be asked. I think it might be one of the first questions asked! Did you belong to my body or not? Did you belong to the false church or the true church? Christ loves His church for which He gave His life. He loves that church so much that He rules everything in this world for the benefit of that church. We must get back to those things said about the church in the Scriptures and what is therefore said about her in the Belgic Confession.

The final words of this chapter give some difficulty. Paul has spoken of the church being Christ's body and then adds "the, fullness of Him that filleth all in all" Let it never be said that Christ is not sufficient unto Himself. Yet, he here speaks of that church being the fullness of HIM, even though He fills all in all. The best interpretation seems to be as follows: Christ is presented here as the head of the church and the church is presented as His body. Keeping this figure in mind, the closing words of this chapter become clear. The head is not complete without the body, and, of course, the body also would not be complete without the head. In other words, the church is here spoken of as complementing the Christ! As Christ, as Messiah, He would not be complete without the church—His body. This again reveals the importance of the church.

Marvelous things have been spoken concerning the salvation of His people in this chapter and the important place of the church. These are the things which he will explain further in the coming chapters of this glorious book.

Questions for Discussion

1. How are faith and love related?
2. According to Paul, the believer sees things the unbeliever does not see. Can there then ever be a true discussion between them?
3. Why do we emphasize so little the power of God in our redemption? Do you think this might make a greater impression on the unbeliever than if we always talk about love?
4. The rule of Christ really began with His ascension. Why do you think believers generally pay so little attention to the Ascension of Christ? If we pay so little attention to it, do we preach a complete gospel?
5. How important is it to which church you belong? Should it be worth going a few extra miles to join one church instead of another? Someone wrote: the church is fellowship. What do you think of that?

Salvation is of the Lord

Ephesians 2:1-10

Surely, anyone who lays claim to the name "Christian"
would agree with the statement that salvation is of the
Lord. That is, he would agree to this statement theoretically.
However, practically, many Christians still believe that the
Lord has made salvation possible and that they now also
have an important role to play in order to receive this
salvation.

By Nature Dead

In Ephesians 2 it is made crystal clear that man does
nothing in the obtaining of his salvation. *"You were dead!"*
A dead person does not turn, he doesn't believe, he does
nothing! This is perhaps the clearest and strongest statement
found in the Bible to teach us that man is indeed totally
depraved. This is a doctrine which men do not wish to
accept. The passage under consideration here leaves no
room for doubt that if salvation — from beginning to end
— does not come from the Lord, there will be none.

The deadness of which the writer speaks is a spiritual
death. They were dead through their trespasses and sins.
This does not refer to the physical nature in the first place,
but to the fact that in his relationship to God, man died
when he fell into sin. So are we also, able to understand the
words uttered by God in the Garden of Eden — in the day
thou dost eat of this fruit thou shalt surely die. He did!
Man by nature is not able to respond to the voice of God.
This is such an important truth that it must be clearly
understood by everyone. The Heidelberg Catechism asks

which things are necessary for us to know for salvation and it answers that we must first know how great our sin and misery is. If one doesn't know *that*, no other knowledge will be of any value. Paul leaves no room for doubt. How great is man's sin and misery? It killed him spiritually!

The translators seem to have a great difficulty with this statement of Paul. The ASV, for example, even begins with the words: "and you did he make alive." The words "did he make alive" are written in italics which means that these words were not found in the original. The addition of these words seems to be an attempt to give an answer to the questions which might be raised by those reading this epistle. Paul indeed gives this answer to the deepest questions which can be raised regarding man's total inability; but he doesn't give the answer until verse five because he has more to say about this total depravity. His answer is then so much richer than the answer of those who were running ahead of the Apostle.

A "Dead" Life

It must again be emphasized that the Apostle is speaking concerning their former *spiritual* death, because he now speaks of the fact that they "walked according to the course of this world." It was possible for these who were dead to walk! But, only according to the course of this world, which lies in the midst of death. They enjoyed themselves in that environment. It was in keeping with their whole outlook. They lived in that sin. They were obedient to the prince of the powers of the air. The writer means the prince of darkness. He inhabits this world and the atmosphere surrounding it. His is a mighty power — though not supreme. But, these people felt at home in this world of sin and were satisfied to follow the evil one wherever he would lead them. If you want to know what that was like, says Paul, then look at the lives of those around you who hate

God and have sold themselves to Satan. That is the kind of
a life you formerly lived! He calls them "sons of
disobedience." To obey anyone above them is totally foreign
to them. They are the offspring of disobedience!

But, one must not conclude that the state of sin in which
they had been was any different from the state of sin of
others. No, *we all* once lived that kind of life. He includes
himself among such sinners. All boasting is excluded! By
nature all once "lived in the lusts of the flesh, doing the
desires of the flesh and mind" — of course! Why would
anyone who is spiritually dead live any other way? But,
remember, we were then the children of wrath even as all
those who know not the Lord.

Made Alive With Christ

Although Paul pictures the desperate condition of natural
man most clearly, he also shows the beauty of salvation as
clearly as it can be put in human language. Man was dead
by nature and could therefore do nothing to relieve his
condition — but God entered into his condition. The mercy
of God is revealed. The love of God (to those who were
children of wrath) rescued those who were dead. He did not
love them because they were so good and so obedient but
He loved them while they were dead! How can a person
believe in a salvation and not believe in election! He chose
those who were dead! He made us alive together with
Christ! That's the answer to the mystery of the passage.
Following the original order we see the riches of salvation
so much more clearly than if we run ahead of the writer
and say already in the first verse of this chapter "and you
did he make alive." Don't try to improve on the language
and thought of the Scriptures!

The parenthetical statement which we find at the close of
verse five is indeed significant. "By grace ye are saved."
This ought to be clear to everyone, that it is the grace of

God and that grace alone which saves us. Salvation is indeed of the Lord. He lifted us up while we were dead and gave us life in Christ, Who is the only source of life. He then raised us up with Him and even made us to sit in the heavenly places with Him. From death to life; from poverty to riches; from the lowliest station to the highest! Christians suffered with Him, they will also be glorified in Him; they died with Him, they will also be raised to life in Him.

A Progressing Discovery

Verse seven almost seems to be somewhat out of tune with that which has gone before and therefore there are also many fanciful interpretations of this verse. However, Paul is very logical in this statement. All of that which is given us in our salvation, or all that is given to us in Christ, is not immediately evident. Every day of our lives unfolds more of the riches which have been given us in Him. That is all that he means by the ages to come. It is in all future time — both now and in eternity that the fullness of our salvation will be unfolded. That grace is so great that the Apostle as it were coins another word ("the exceeding riches of his grace") in order to make plain to the church what wealth she has received.

God's Gift of Faith

In verse eight we have perhaps one of the most beautiful summaries of the Christian faith and also the most comprehensive. Once more Paul repeats the fact that Christians have been saved by grace. Salvation was effected through faith. Now, is not that faith our contribution toward that salvation? He gives immediate reply: "and that not of yourselves, it is the gift of God." Saved by grace? Indeed. Wrought by faith? Indeed. But, even that faith which God's people exercise is His gift! Salvation is indeed of the Lord and we do not add one iota to it. This is the emphasis of this whole passage and is of the greatest importance for understanding the nature, not only of salvation, but later in this same epistle, also the nature of the church. In our own circles we often read of "accepting Christ," "deciding for Christ" etc. Is this bad? We know what is meant. We must speak the language of Scripture! No one who is dead "accepts" Christ or "decides" for Him. When we use the language which is common in the evangelical world, but is contrary to the language of Scripture, we minimize the grace of God. The exceeding riches of His grace must always be celebrated.

Not Saved By Good Works

To make it clear that all the emphasis must rest on the grace of God and salvation as a free gift, he adds the words: "not of works that no man should glory." The Jews were always tempted to seek their eternal welfare, not entirely, but, nevertheless in part, in their good works. Then a man has something in which he can glory. He has accomplished something. Paul is not writing primarily to the Jews in this epistle but to those who have come out of the gentile world. But, this makes no difference. It is not only a characteristic of the Jew to embrace good works which he has done — it is the difficulty with which every human being strives. It takes a great deal of grace to live on grace! Jesus struck at the very heart of this matter when he told His followers that they would have to deny themselves and so follow Him. The self is the last person we want to deny. The gospel of Jesus Christ has made us fabulously rich but it has robbed us of all self-glorying. Yet, what would be man's own glorying? What does he possess whereof he may glory? The only thing he can claim as his own is his sin! Let those who glory, glory in the Lord Who has raised them from death to life and will give them so much in the time to come that it is beyond their ability to imagine.

Saved For Good Works

No sooner has the Apostle warned the readers against basing their hope for salvation on their works, than he begins to speak of the good works which the believer must do. In fact, those who have tasted of the redeeming grace of God are His workmanship. There is nothing in them which they owe to anyone but Him. He made them what they are. Now, in Christ Jesus He has created this workmanship for a purpose and the purpose is good works. In the churches of the Reformation there was some hesitancy to do justice to the Scriptural teaching concerning good works. They had seen the evil of an emphasis on such works becoming a misinterpretation of salvation as man's doing. But, although the doctrine is fraught with all manner of difficulty, it may not be ignored because it is the clear teaching of Scripture that good works are to be done. That's what God saved them for. God even prepared these works so that we should walk in them. The life of good works is therefore to be the climate of the redeemed life. Now, how does this differ from the works which Paul warned against in the previous verse? There the works were considered as those which might aid in the salvation of the individuals performing them. That, says Paul, is out of the question. Salvation is by grace alone. However, that redeemed life will bear a certain stamp and will be different from the unredeemed. The different life is what God redeemed us *for*. The mode of life must now correspond to His will, out of gratitude for the salvation which has been received. If life be viewed as a tree, the natural man wants to place his own works among the roots of that tree. The Scriptures teach that the good works of believers are found in the *fruit* of such a tree. Believers must bring forth fruit. That which is fruitless, barren, is good for nothing but is removed from its place. So important are these good works, that we are to walk in them, and that it may even be said that there is no salvation apart from them.

Questions for discussion:

1. Is Paul going too far when he says that the natural man is dead in trespasses and sins? Is that your experience with unbelievers?

2. Is it all right to sing: "I have decided to follow Jesus?" Is it all right to speak of "accepting Christ?" What's wrong with it? Is it harmless?

3. God chose His people and gave them life even while they were dead in trespasses and sins. He also speaks of "children of wrath." Who are they? Is it proper to say to everyone "God loves you"?

4. Why do the Scriptures call us to faith and obedience, seeing these things are the gift of God? Why does the Bible call me to repent when only He can make me repent?

5. Why is the whole matter of good works a "touchy" question? Can you understand why the Heidelberg Catechism brings up the subject three times?

Jew and Gentile Brought Together

Ephesians 2:11-17

Jewish Privileges

One of the greatest problems confronting the New Testament church was: How can gentiles also be admitted to the church of Jesus Christ? Surely, you cannot negate thousands of years of history and all the gifts which had been bestowed on one people (the Jews) and say that we now start on an equal footing! Does it mean nothing that the Jews were the beloved of God? Does it mean nothing that the Jews have served the true God for thousands of years? Does it mean nothing that the promises had been given to the Jews? Does it mean nothing that God had given His laws only to this people?

When one considers the above questions he realizes that it was nothing short of revolutionary to bring the gospel of Jesus Christ to the gentiles. The Jews had been brought up to recognize the gentiles as "dogs." The covenant had been given to the Jews, and to the Jews only, and its sign was circumcision. The gentiles were therefore commonly referred to as the uncircumcised. That made it clear enough to everyone that they were different people with whom the Jews would have nothing to do. Woes had been pronounced on those who would marry outside of the people of God. Jews were not even permitted to eat with gentiles. They were the unclean. And now God says "How dare you call common what I have made clean!" This naturally raised difficult questions for the sincere Jew. Something had already been done before Ephesians was written to make clear that a new era had dawned. The Synod of Jerusalem had been held and "officially" the relationship between Jew and gentile Christians had been established. But, this decision spoke of some ethical principles: the gentiles should not eat of things sacrificed to idols; they should not eat of the flesh with the blood; they should not eat that which had been strangled; and they should (of course) abstain from fornication. Is that all that is now required in this New Testament time? What about circumcision? What about the rules and regulations concerning diet? Has everything now become *easy*? Let non-discrimination be an official position — practice will dictate something else! Even the Apostle Peter found it difficult to *swallow* this view and was criticized severely by Paul (Gal. 2:llff.).

Paul does give us a little insight into the hypocrisy of the Jews concerning their relation to the gentiles when he speaks of a "circumcision made by hands." Of course, this was the only circumcision which existed, but, his emphasis on the fact that it was made by hands shows us that with many it was only an external rite. Then the circumcision, of course, was meaningless and was not a sign (a true sign) of the covenant of grace. It must be borne in mind that all that which was circumcised was not automatically the true people of God.

Gentile Privations

But, let it also be clear that something great had to happen to these gentiles before they could be accounted to belong to God's people. When the Jews had accused them of being uncircumcised, they had been far removed from God. They were without Christ, and there is no salvation apart from Him. They had been a people which was wretched. The Jew had looked for a Savior to come, while the gentiles didn't even recognize their need of a Savior.

They had also been "alienated from the commonwealth of Israel." Of course — they had their own state and their own government. Was this a serious lack on their part that they did not belong to the commonwealth of Israel? Yes it was. Israelites had a Theocracy — God was their Ruler. He had given them His laws so that the Apostle can say at another occasion: What nation has such laws as Israel? Israel was highly privileged to have this kind of government. The gentiles were aliens to all of this. Their own governments were usually corrupt and ruled for themselves.

They had also been "strangers from the covenants of the promise." If there was one outstanding element in the relationship of God to His chosen people, it was the fact that he had made His covenant with them. In this covenant He had promised to be their God. What that meant in all its depth was not fully known until Christ came. But, it was a covenant of friendship which He had made with His people. That the plural, "covenants," is used seems to indicate only that the same covenant was reiterated time and again throughout the Old Testament history. This covenant is not between equals nor is it an agreement in which both parties have the same importance. Man must accept it by faith, but God makes the covenant. How richly Israel had been blessed through this relationship, and the gentiles were simply strangers to this relationship.

Being strangers to God's covenant, they were, of course, without hope in this life. If He is not their God and they are not His people, there is no hope! What a hopeless world the gospel came into. Idolatry brings fear — but no hope!

Paul concludes this list of the things which the gentiles lacked by stating that they were "without God in the world." The gentiles had their own gods and thereby they tried to satisfy their basic need. But they failed. These idols were not able to instill any hope and gave no comfort to those who worshiped them. The true God had made them and had also given them many things. But, they did not have the knowledge of the true God nor of the way of salvation.

From all of this it becomes evident that the plight of the gentiles was a desperate one. They had nothing. Are these now to be placed on the same plane with the Jews who have been so highly favored? Isn't the salvation brought by Christ the natural property of the Jews? How can these hated gentiles suddenly become their brothers?

Christ's Reconciliation

The miracle has occurred through the coming of Christ into this world and the work He has accomplished. That which seemed to be a total impossibility has become a fact. The gentiles were so far removed from God. Christ has drawn them close. The blood of Christ has accomplished wonders. Now the blood of Christ has first of all brought God and the sinner together. This is the salvation of which the Bible speaks. But, He has done far more by the sacrifice which He has brought. He has not only brought God and man together, He has also brought man and man together, and therefore also the Jew and the gentile. He is the One who has established peace where there was enmity. He has made both one! There had been a wall between them which nothing and nobody seemed to be able to break down. That hostility grew with the years. Christ broke down this wall. Here in Ephesus one can see the effect of the work of Christ. Jew and gentile are worshipping together and sit at the same table. The Bible knows of only one division — believer and unbeliever, no Jew and gentile or any other distinction. Christ broke down barriers and brought men together as well as reconciling them with their God.

How did Christ accomplish the deed of bringing Jew and gentile together? He "abolished in His flesh the enmity, even the law of commandments contained in ordinances." What does this mean? The Apostle is not speaking of the moral law or the law of the ten commandments. Those will always stand and will have to be observed by both Jew and gentile. No, it is rather the ceremonial law which he has in mind. The Jew could not understand that those who had always been his enemies could now receive all the benefits of salvation in Christ. On the other hand, the gentile could not understand how circumcision would benefit him in his salvation. He could not understand how the failure to eat pork could help him in his salvation. This does not mean that this ceremonial law had never been of value. It had taught Israel much during the Old Testament times. It showed that God's people was a peculiar people. They were to be separated from all others. But, that time is past. Christ has in His flesh abolished this ceremonial law. He has brought the great sacrifice and don't let anyone bring another sin offering! Israel had fallen into the error of placing the ceremonial law above the moral, and this had led it to a mere formal religion. This is done away. Let those who worship God worship in spirit and in truth, whether they be Jew or gentile.

In this way Christ has created "in Himself of the two one new man, so making peace." Only the sacrificial work of Christ was able to accomplish that which no one else had ever accomplished. Faith in Jesus Christ as the only Savior of men is the only requirement for both Jew and gentile. Therein they have become the same. Both Jew and gentile have received great riches through the Christ of God.

United in Christ's Church

So has Christ reconciled men to God and has formed that body called the church. The church of Jesus Christ is a marvel in this world. That is the only body in which old and young, rich and poor, and all races meet and call one another brethren. We must never lose sight of the fact that *the one holy catholic church is an article of faith*! Who could ever have imagined that such a body could come into existence after sin had entered the world? We see it but we don't understand it. The glory of that body, the church, is emphasized in Ephesians as nowhere else. How is it possible that people can speak so lightly of the church which is His body and believe that they have made a great improvement on the message of Scripture by always speaking of a personal Savior and a personal salvation. Of course these statements are true; but only in the light of the church, the body, the bride of Jesus Christ! He builds His church. He gives His life for His church. Many of the ills, spiritual ills, of the present day can be traced to a faulty conception of the church. When true and false church are no longer "easily distinguished" from each other, there is trouble. When it is emphasized that no church has all of the truth — one may conclude that there is no true church, and we then call on such vague concepts as an invisible church!

Christ has established peace through the work which He accomplished. This peace is now found between Jew and gentile. However, such a peace will never come unless they are both reconciled to God. The relationship to God must be right before there will ever be the possibility of a proper relationship between men. He Himself preached that peace. Never did anyone speak as He spoke. He came with the gospel — the good news. He preached it not to one group, but to all. He preached it to those who were nigh, who were close — the Jews. He also spoke it to those who were far off — the gentiles. This was the true gospel. This brought peace of heart and that only is the true peace. He restored hope. He gave meaning to life. He accomplished what the prophets of the Old Testament attempted — to turn the people from formalism to the true religion. Great peace have they who follow Him. He is our peace. He is the

Prince of peace. He preached it and the church must preach that same message.

Questions for discussion:

1. Does the ceremonial law have anything to teach us today? How about Israel's civil law?
2. Why was there such hostility between Jew and gentile? Does that still exist? Is there any way of preventing another holocaust, such as that in the 1940s, except by means of the preaching of the Word?
3. Seeing faith in Jesus Christ is all that is necessary, is it very important to speak of the covenant and all the other things summed up by
   Paul in vs. 12? Is there the danger today that we ignore such things as the covenant and only emphasize the necessity of believing in Jesus?
4. We are indebted to the blood of Christ for our salvation. For anything else?
5. Why is the church an article of faith? Do we sufficiently emphasize the importance of being the true church and belonging to that church only?
6. What determines whether or not a church is the true church?

Lesson 5

Jew and Gentile – Fellow Citizens

Ephesians 2:19-22

We must remember that the description which Paul had given of the state of the gentiles in contrast with that of the Jews before the gospel came to Ephesus was one of which they were not even aware at that time. The unbeliever doesn't realize what he is missing and can, seemingly, be quite happy in his life separated from God and from His people. The Spirit of God must open the eyes to make one see the poverty of such a state and fill him with a "holy jealousy" for what the people of God enjoy. Those things have happened in Ephesus. They have been brought together, Jew and gentile, through the power of the work of Christ. He was the only one who could effect a reconciliation between the two. He has sent His Spirit to complete the work He began, and in the church Jew and gentile may and can now call one another brothers!

Former Strangers

Before this the gentiles were strangers to the household of God. They had not even heard of him. The proselyting during the Old Testament dispensation must have been very limited. There are a few names in the Old Testament which show us that this "mission work" was not completely absent. There is a Ruth and there is a Rahab. These, despite the obstacles thrown in their path, were assimilated into the people of God. But, who had heard of the God of Abraham in the Greek and Roman world of Paul's day? The Jews had remained strangers among the people in whose lands they dwelt! It is therefore not too much to say that the gentiles were strangers to the household of God.

The Great Change

But, all of this has changed. The change which has come with the coming of Jesus Christ into the world cannot be measured. Now, all of a sudden, it makes no difference whether you are born a Jew or a Greek; the all-important question is: Do you believe on the Son of God? The Ephesians had believed on Him. Then you are no longer strangers to the household of God! No, you then have become *members* of that household. Those who have come at the eleventh hour (Matthew 20) receive the same wages as those who were in the field since early morning! The Jew can't understand this. Is God fair in dealing alike with both? Not if it is a matter of earning. One certainly ought to earn more in twelve hours than in one. But, it is not a matter of earning — it is *grace*, and grace is not measured in terms of time. This was a difficult lesson for the Jew to learn. In fact, it was so difficult a lesson that they condemned the gospel and the gospel ministers for it!

Now Citizens

Not only has the status of strangers been removed from these gentiles since they believed, they are also not to be considered as mere sojourners. The latter were privileged above strangers. They had a place with the saints. The Gibeonites, for example, lived among the Israelites for years and benefited greatly by this contact. But, they were not citizens! Israel had to "put up with them" because of the vow made to their fathers by Joshua. Let not the church of the New Testament take that attitude toward these people who have come to the faith in Jesus Christ even though their roots are in the gentile world. What a privilege to be fellow-citizens with the saints and of the household of God. It is one of the author's purposes to make clear to these people how favored they are.

The Well Founded Building

From the term "household" he easily progresses to the idea of an edifice or house of which they have become a part. They have become citizens of a structure which is of the greatest significance. It is "built on the foundation of the apostles and prophets." This, of course, does not mean that these apostles and prophets "themselves" were the foundation on which this structure rested. It was rather the teaching of both apostles and prophets which formed the foundation of the house of which they were now members. Again, Paul does not refer to the prophets of the Old Testament, but to those of the New. These were secondary to the apostles but they, nevertheless, brought the same gospel, the same foundational message. The church is built on this foundation and on no other. Now there are those who teach that Christ is the foundation of the church. This is, of course, true (I Cor. 3:11). But, when the apostles and prophets come with the word of Christ, it can just as well be said that they are the foundation of the church. Similar expressions are found elsewhere. Christ is the Light of the world; but He also says that His followers are the light of the world. Ephesus must realize that the Christ is speaking through apostles and prophets. They come with the authoritative word. To look at them only as servants of the people is to attack the foundation of the church.

"The Chief Cornerstone"

But what is the role which Christ plays in the establishment and continuance of this building? Paul says that Christ Jesus Himself is "the chief cornerstone." This is not the first time the Scriptures have spoken of cornerstones

and of Christ being a cornerstone. Psalm 118:22
immediately comes to mind. There are various passages in
the New Testament which refer to this passage and show
the important place Christ has in the structure of the
church. Yet, I find it very difficult to understand all these
various passages in their specific meaning. I also believe that
the term "cornerstone" is not always used in the same sense
in Scripture. Sometimes it indeed refers to part of the
foundation, while at other times it seems to refer more to
what we today call "a key stone." When we speak of a
cornerstone today we mean neither the one nor the other.
At a "cornerstone laying" it is not a part of the foundation
which is put in place, but, rather, a special stone with an
inscription, etc. — one which could also be missed from the
building. The question now becomes: In what sense is the
term used in this particular text? The text seems to leave no
doubt that by it is meant the most important part of the
foundation. It is that stone which determines the angle of
the walls and binds the walls together. When they are built
on the foundation of apostles and prophets, they are also
built on the foundation which is Jesus Christ. These truths
are fundamental for the understanding of the nature of the
church our Lord has come to build here on this earth. He,
together with the teaching of His apostles and prophets are
the basis upon which it stands. Outside of the church there
is no salvation. (Article 28, Belgic Confession) The writer
immediately does away with that atomistic view of
salvation which is proclaimed so much today. The
importance of the church is now being lost from view.
Many still speak endearingly of Jesus but will have nothing
to do with the teaching of the apostles and prophets. This is
the characteristic of the false church.

The Building Which "Grows"
    The first part of vs. 21 should not be translated "in whom

each several building," etc.; but, "in whom the entire building," etc. There is but one church and the context had also made it clear that he was speaking of only one house which was being built. It is necessary that a firm foundation shall be laid for any house. The previous verse shows that the church has such a foundation. As I have stated before, Paul struggles with the limitations of human language. He has been speaking of a building. This, everyone can understand. When it comes to the foundation of that building he already makes it more difficult for us to understand him, but now, when he is speaking of the superstructure, logic seems to break down. That this description is a harmonious whole, we expect. The Master Builder is at work. Everything fits. But Paul goes on to say that this building, "groweth into a holy temple in the Lord." The building which sounded very much like a house when he first began to speak of it, now *grows* into a *temple*. This building, small at first, grows into something very large. This building, not esteemed highly at first, grows into a temple or sanctuary. A *building* that *grows*, is of course, materially impossible. But, when the apostle is speaking of the work of Christ, when he is speaking of the church of Christ, there is no metaphor which is capable of giving the whole picture. Christ has built His church. The teachings of apostles and prophets form its foundation. But, there is nothing static about the work of Christ. It throbs with life! Wherever one touches His work he is brought in contact with the only true life. Now, how can this be revealed in a "building?" The "building" itself will have to "grow" in order to adequately portray Christ's church. Notice what it grows into — a *temple*, a sanctuary. It grows into a holy place. The work of God has great "success." That which began so small and so insignificant has become something of surpassing beauty and of great value.

Living Members

Not only does Paul speak of the church in general terms; he now also tells these Ephesians what their place is in this temple of God. They are the "living stones" of which the Apostle Peter speaks. When they come in contact with the foundation or with the cornerstone, they become alive! That is the reason this building can grow. It is made up of living building material. Each individual believer has his own place in this temple. All together they form then this temple or sanctuary in which God dwells by His Spirit! God lives in the church! That is His proper abode. The temple in Jerusalem was only a type. The building of that temple, Solomon, was well aware of this. The heavens are not able to contain Him — then how shall a house made with dead building material ever be able to house Him? Something better would have to come eventually. In 70 A.D. the temple in Jerusalem, which Herod had built, was destroyed. That was all right. It had served its purpose. The church had been founded and that is the place where God makes His abode.

God's Living House

It is the habitation of God in the Spirit. The spiritual nature of God's dwelling place was easy to overlook in the Old Testament times. God dwelt — first in the tabernacle and then in the temple. The Holy of Holies was the place where He dwelt in a very special manner. Only the high priest was allowed to enter there, and then only once a year. The heathen too had their temples. In Ephesus they had the great temple of Diana and her likeness within it. Israel's temple contained a *box*! Surely, they would not fall down before that in worship! Now God lives in the Spirit in the church where everything is alive! You are that temple!

Questions for discussion:

1. Does the gospel first make men dissatisfied with their lives? Explain. What do you think of the idea of building on something which the unbeliever already has?

2. Do we fully appreciate our relationship to the church of Christ? Do you think there would be so much criticism of the church if we did?

3. What does it mean that Christ was made the head of the corner?

4. Catholicism believes in the direct descent of apostolic authority to the clergy of the present day. Protestants have been afraid of this view. Why? Have we lost something vital and precious as a result?

5. If a minister used illustrations the way Paul did, do you think it would be helpful in understanding his thought? Explain.

Paul Makes Known the Mystery of Redemption

Ephesians 3:1-13

In this epistle Paul deals, of course, with the glorious gospel of Jesus Christ and its value for all those who believe. However, he does not just repeat himself in each epistle. There are certain emphases in the one epistle which are not found in the others. In this letter he deals with the *church* of Christ, the blessing of being a member of that glorious body of our Lord, and he magnifies the office which has been given him. These are very important considerations for the church of our day. Many no longer realize what is Biblically meant by the term "church" and there is much confusion regarding office.

Christ's Prisoner

Paul begins this chapter in a strange way. The first verse forms an incomplete sentence. This is not completed in the immediately following verses, but one has to go all the way to verse 14 to find the conclusion of the thought he had begun to express in verse 1. He refers to all that he has written in the previous two chapters when he begins, "For this cause." He is a prisoner at this time and that for a very definite reason. They must not look on him as one who deserves incarceration for crimes committed. He is "a prisoner of Christ Jesus in behalf of you Gentiles." He is not ashamed of the fact that he is in prison in Rome. One will usually seek to hide the fact that he has been in prison at one time or another, but Paul doesn't. It is amazing how often he brings up this rather touchy subject. He was imprisoned because he has been faithful! Those who did not proclaim the full gospel of Jesus Christ have their freedom. He has made known the whole counsel of God — and that brings trouble! It is because of these gentiles that he is in prison. He has claimed an equal place for them with the believing Jews — and that brought trouble! He has to defend his apostleship time and again. Let no man say that his imprisonment is an indication that he is not a true apostle. He is Christ's prisoner. He is a prisoner because he was faithful to his calling. If anything, the fact that he is a prisoner is an indication that he is truly an apostle!

There are various translations current of the words found in verse 2. As this verse is translated in the ASV, it is difficult to understand what the author has in mind. However, he is not speaking of a dispensation, but of a "stewardship," or of a manner in which Paul has dealt with that grace of God which had been given him as a trust and which he was to use for their benefit. The "if" is not an indication of uncertainty, but ought to be understood as meaning "since." These Ephesians had heard the gospel very clearly from the mouth of Paul. They also knew that he had spent himself for the gospel and for those who were the recipients of the gospel.

The "Mystery"

That whole gospel was the "mystery." It was that which had not been made known before but was now revealed. This he had received by *revelation*. It was not a philosophy of men. It had not been given to him by others. He had received it directly from his God. He was an apostle! God had spoken to him. What he had made known to the Ephesian church was not some "cunningly devised fable," it was the word of God Himself. They must, therefore, recognize Paul as God's trustee. He had been entrusted with the word of God. He had made known to them things which prophets and even angels did not understand! Let them then see how exalted was the office to which he had been called — who was now a prisoner. Then they would be able to pray for him and they would also gladly hear God's word from him. He told them that he had referred to this matter before very briefly. They must never lose sight of the content of this mystery and they must also remember from whom they had heard it.

Revealed to Paul

As they read this epistle his understanding of the gospel, or of the mystery, will become clear to them. Is this pride? Paul has been accused of pride by many throughout the ages. He speaks of the fact that his labors have been more productive than those of other apostles, etc. So here, he writes, "You will be able to see how well I understand the gospel." However, in verse 8 the humility of this man is clearly shown. No, there is no false pride, but, rather, complete honesty! And, the understanding he has of this mystery is indeed profound. Who has so delved into the depths of the gospel of Jesus Christ as he? Who has shown such riches in the gospel as he? Yet, this is not of his own doing but is the gift of God.

Previously Hidden

In verse five the apostle again emphasizes the fact that the mystery of which he has been speaking has not been made known in previous generations. However, he still has not defined the nature of this mystery. It is indeed that which has now been revealed to the apostles and the prophets of the New Testament dispensation. And now, in verse six, he tells us what the content of that mystery is. The fact that it had not been made known to previous generations must not

lead us to the conclusion that the prophets of the Old
Testament had not spoken at all about the future relation of
Jew and gentile. There are many passages which speak of
the blessing which is going to come to the gentile through
the Jew. However, they did not know *how* this would come
to pass, nor did they know the *nature* of the blessing which
the gentile would receive. This is now revealed.

Entry of the Gentiles

The Old Testament prophets leave the impression that
somehow the gentiles must be united to Israel in order to
receive Israel's blessing. God had made a covenant with His
people — an everlasting covenant. Somehow the gentiles
must be brought into that relationship; but how? The Spirit
had made it clear that a *new humanity* had come into being
with the coming of Jesus Christ. The theocracy falls away
and the church of the New Testament comes into being.
Now the gentiles can become fellow-heirs (if ye be Christ's,
ye are Abraham's seed). They have become fellow-members
of the same body — which is the church. They have
therefore become fellow partakers of the promise in Christ
— of eternal salvation. The whole manner of life has been
changed. History has changed. Even the apostles had
difficulty understanding this change. You can see the
understanding this particular apostle has in this mystery of
Jesus Christ. He grasped it!

Paul's Privilege

This mystery, then, has been made known in the gospel,
and of that gospel, says Paul, I was made a minister! What
a privilege! He is honored above the great of the Old
Testament times. He is not self-appointed. No, it was a gift
of God that he was made a minister. How gracious his God
has been. It is also the power of God which has worked
through the gospel which he was allowed to proclaim.

He isn't worthy of this honor. He is "less than the least of all saints." In other places he speaks in similar language. In I Cor. 15 he says that he is the least of the apostles. In I Tim. 1 he says that he is the chief of sinners. He cannot understand that to him has been given such a blessing that he may make known to the gentiles the unsearchable riches of Christ. This is a gospel which goes far beyond the understanding of men. It is so beautiful! Gladly will he suffer for this Christ and for His gospel. It is the greatest news ever made known.

God's Revelation

The purpose of the ministry of the gospel is to enlighten everyone how this salvation, this mystery, now works. Christ is the content of the gospel and He is the One who will bring the true light to all those who believe that gospel. These things were formerly hidden from the eyes of men, they were hidden in God. If He had not revealed Himself, no one would ever have known Him, for no one can by searching find out God. So also concerning the salvation of both Jew and gentile — it had to be revealed! Only He who had created all things could reveal it.

"Many-colored Wisdom"

The purpose of making known this gospel is also found even beyond the present sphere. It is to make known to the principalities and powers, i.e., to angels, the glorious wisdom of God. The word translated *manifold* doesn't do justice to the original. Paul really speaks of the multi-splendored, the multicolored, wisdom of God! This is made known through the church. It is true that all His works praise Him and that all things reveal His wisdom, but the church reflects that wisdom in a manner found nowhere else. These are things angels desire to look into. Therefore, proclaim the true gospel so that the true church may come into being and the glorious wisdom of God will be revealed to them.

God's Eternal Purpose

The eternal purpose of the God who created all things is summed up in Christ Jesus our Lord. All God's works have purpose. Christ stands at the center of them all. In Him will God's glorious wisdom be revealed. John speaks of the fact that this Word was from eternity; that He became flesh; and that He will come again as judge. God's full purpose has not yet been realized. There is more to come but it will all center in the Christ.

Benefits Realized

This Christ, Who is our Lord, has given Himself for these to whom the Apostle is writing. They must realize what benefits have been bestowed on them in Him. In Him they have a boldness to come to God. They are children who have freedom of speech before their Father. This gives them confidence. All of life has been changed. Faith in Jesus Christ has brought life to light.

Confidence

Seeing these Ephesians have received so much through the gospel which has come to them and which has been believed by them, nothing must blind them to the glorious grace revealed. They are aware, of course, that Paul is in prison in Rome, and he has spoken of this himself. They must not become downcast as a result of the situation. Regardless what comes in life, we may not become discouraged. He shows that he is confident that the sufferings of the present time are not to be compared to the glory which is ours. The church in Ephesus feels badly about Paul's imprisonment. He could do so much if he were free. He asks them not to look at his suffering in that way. He will glory in tribulation — and they must too!

He, Whose purposes cannot be thwarted, is in control. He realizes all His purposes in Christ Jesus. The future is in good hands!

Questions for discussion:

1. What is Paul's view of his calling? In Galatians 1 he also mentions the fact that he had received his message by revelation. Therefore he is fully aware of the fact that he is proclaiming the word of God. How can a present day minister be certain that he is proclaiming the word of God?

2. Do you think Paul saw more clearly and earlier than the others that the gentiles were fellow heirs of salvation? Why? Remember he was a Pharisee.

3. Did Paul have too high a view of his ministry? Can we have too high a view of it today?

4. Does the church today reflect the wisdom of God? Does your church?

5. What is Christ's position in history?

6. If we understand the gospel and truly believe it, can we ever complain?

Paul's Prayer for the Ephesian Church

Ephesians 3:14-21

The main task which the Lord has given the apostles to do is to teach and proclaim the glorious gospel of Jesus Christ. However, there was also a priestly work to be done to build up the church which the Lord had established. It is clear from all his writings that Paul engages in prayer for the church constantly. His prayers are found throughout his writings. Many times when he is in the midst of an important point of doctrine he suddenly offers his thanksgiving to the God Whom he serves, for the wonders of His revelation. He also assures his readers again and again that he is remembering them before the throne of God.

The thought introduced in verse 1 of this chapter is now, finally, taken up in verse 14 and following verses. At the beginning of this chapter he says: "For this cause I Paul, the prisoner of Christ Jesus in behalf of you gentiles," but the thought is not completed! How typically Pauline! There were other things he had to make clear to them, namely, that there was no longer a separation between Jew and gentile, but that they had been brought together in Christ. Now, in verse 14 he takes up that which he had begun to say in verse 1. He bows his knees before God the Father, for this cause. What is the cause? That Jew and gentile have been brought together! The marvel of the gospel! Because of that he bows his knees before the Father. He is awed by the great responsibility and the great blessing which has been

given him that he has been made a minister of such a
gospel. Notice that "the Father" is always the One to
Whom he prays.

To the Father of the Family
  The whole family in heaven and on earth is named after
Him. By this whole family he means the household of God,
the church of Jesus Christ. This is a family which is not
only found here on earth but is found in heaven too. Those
who have fallen asleep in Jesus belong to the church which
we usually call "the church triumphant." It is that part of
the church which is beyond the strife and suffering of the
church here. It (the church) includes, of course, Jew and
gentile. Not only the church militant and the church
triumphant, but he even seems to include the angel host in
this "whole family." It is true that the angels are not
recipients of salvation through the blood of Christ and that
they are not bound together with bonds of blood as men
are. Yet, these also are part of the family of God. They are
servants who have been taken into the household. We
should pay far more attention to the things the Scriptures
teach us about the angels than we usually do.

For the Spirit's Powers
  Now he reveals the content of his prayer. He prays that
God the Father may give them this blessing that they may
be strengthened with power through His Spirit in the
inward man. He prays that all the powers of God (riches of
His glory) may be given the believer for the strengthening of
his faith. He prays that all the attributes of God may be
applied to his spiritual progress. So often men speak only of
such things as the grace, mercy and love of God which are
to be given for our spiritual well-being. Paul speaks of all
the riches of God to be used for this end. The Spirit of God
uses all the attributes of God to strengthen faith within us.

For that strengthening we need His Almighty power as well as His grace. We need His changelessness as well as His love. Then we are truly strengthened! Then the inward man, i.e., the heart is made strong. This fact is spoken of by the Apostle time and again in his epistles. He does not "play off" the one attribute of God against another. All of them are to be honored in our salvation. Consequently, we will speak of more than the love or the grace of God when we praise Him for our redemption. All of His powers are at our disposal, and we impoverish ourselves when we do not recognize this fact.

For Christ's Indwelling

The above is necessary to recognize and believe in order that Christ may dwell in your hearts through faith. He makes His abode within the believer through the Spirit. Then we are strong in the faith. The Spirit of God dispenses the power of God. So do we lay hold of it. As a result you will be rooted and grounded in love. Here Paul is using a double figure of speech. That faith of the believer is like a tree having roots into the true nourishment for the life they must feed. It is also like a building which is standing on a foundation of solid rock so that it will always be a safe refuge. This is the picture of that true faith in God wrought by the Spirit and founded on the work of Christ! No one shall ever be able to overthrow that faith. It is not dependent on the one who is exercising it, no, it has its roots, it has its foundation in the love of God! All His attributes stand guard over the faith He has instilled!

Grasping What Is Beyond Knowledge

In this way the believers will also be strong to grasp, together with all other believers, what is the breadth and length and height and depth.... Of what? He doesn't say. The context makes it clear, however, what he has in mind.

It is the breadth and length and height and depth of the love of Christ! Then we naturally ask the question: Who will ever be able to grasp the fullness of the love of Christ? It is limitless, isn't it? The Apostle is fully aware of this too and therefore uses these four terms. He also states that it cannot be grasped by the individual believer, but must be done in the union of all believers. The love of Christ cannot be measured in breadth or length or height or depth. It certainly cannot be grasped by the mind of man. If it is to be grasped at all it will be by faith, by a heart knowledge. But, there is that faith given to man so that he *begins* to grasp something of that limitless love of Christ! He cannot describe it. He cannot fathom it. But, he experiences it! Only when a person has been so strengthened by the power of the Spirit of God is there the possibility that he will be able, in a measure, to grasp the beauty and glory of the heart of his redemption. It is indeed a love which passes knowledge. No unbeliever can understand even the smallest part of it.

Filled to God's Fullness

At the conclusion of this prayer Paul asks that they may be filled unto all the fullness of God. The Bible speaks in many ways of our relationship to God. We are to walk with Him. We are to believe on Him. We are to obey Him. We are to approach to Him in prayer. We are to live for Him, etc. Here the Apostle speaks of being filled to all the fullness of God. So that we may be like Him. We are so to grasp the broad extent of the love of Christ that we may be filled unto all the fullness of God. In other words, we are to be filled to that fullness only through our relationship to Jesus Christ. As we increase in the knowledge of the love of Christ, we are being filled to the fullness of God. This is the way in which the author speaks of true spiritual growth in the believer. It is a growth which is never complete. This is

true because the breadth and length and height and depth of
the love of Christ shall never be fully grasped and because
the fullness of God is limitless! Physical growth is limited to
a certain amount of time. Perhaps this is also true of the
growth of intellect. However, spiritual growth goes on. Nor
is it limited to this life! We are going to grow spiritually
throughout all eternity! Man, even the one who is redeemed
by the blood of Christ, is and remains a creature and no
creature shall ever be able to comprehend the love of Christ
or the fullness of God! Shall such a redeemed person then
not be complete and perfect? When a man is filled with the
fullness of God — is there room for more? When a
container is full — how can it be made to hold more? Yet,
this is precisely what the Bible teaches — we will go on
from perfection to perfection. We will have to think of a
container which is able to stretch to receive more. Not as a
container made of wood or steel, but as a container made
of rubber! It has to hold more even though it is full.

To God's Eternal Glory

When the Apostle has come to the close of this beautiful
and very significant prayer, he ends with a doxology. This is
also typically Pauline. He ends with a doxology after a deep
and penetrating analysis of glorious truth (Romans 11) and
he frequently ends prayers and thanksgivings with a
doxology. In fact, one is able to say that Paul's whole life is
a doxology. He has understanding in the mystery which has
now been revealed, as he says earlier in this chapter. He
knows his Lord and his God and this leads him to the
highest level of praise.

To the God of Whom he has spoken, be the glory. To the
One of Whom the whole family in heaven and on earth is
named. To the One who is to fill His people. This is the
One Who is able to do all things; is able to do far more
than our puny minds are able to ask or think. We have so

many requests. Our minds too are filled with all the things we desire — which seem to be endless. Yet, He is able to do so much more — one is not even able to compare what we can ask or think with the ability He has of giving to His people. Paul again coins words to make it possible for him to express himself in such a way that men will understand the power of their God to care for them. He is able to answer the prayers of those in whom He has begun His work of grace. Besides, that grace which they have received will also encourage them to expect all things from Him, even the things which are humanly impossible.

To this God must the glory be given. The church of Jesus Christ shows the glory of its God. Christ Himself, the Head of that church shows the glory of God. Everything must give praise to Him. He is now, through the redeeming work of Christ, acknowledged as God. Those who have not tasted of redemption do not bring homage to Him, but the church must and does do so. This glorifying of the God Who has accomplished all that He decided to do, must go on throughout all the ages of men here on earth, and must go on forever! Never will we have completed our praise of God. We go from strength to strength — from glory to glory — from victory to victory, always praising and glorifying the God Who has revealed Himself to us. Upon this doxology Paul now pronounces his Amen!

Questions for discussion:
1. How are preaching and prayer related? Can there be the one without the other?
2. What is the place of angels in the redemption of man? Why is there no salvation for fallen angels?
3. There would be no salvation if God were not the God of love and of grace. Would there be salvation for us if He were not the Almighty or the Eternal?
4. How great is the love of Christ? If it could be measured would it be enough?
5. What is perfection for the redeemed?
6. We would willingly agree that God can do all things. Do we recognize this sufficiently in our prayers?

Lesson 8

The Unity and Growth of the Church

Ephesians 4:1-16

The end of the previous chapter marks the end of the first part of this epistle, in which the Apostle has given his teaching. Beginning at chapter four he applies the things he has taught. This is Paul's usual mode of procedure.

He who is writing is a prisoner in the Lord and because of the gospel of Jesus Christ. Let these Ephesians and the whole church of Christ of later times realize that he has given everything for the church and for the gospel. He does not bring up his present situation in order to elicit sympathy, but that the people may realize that he is not speaking for his own advantage but that he is driven by his relationship to his Savior. He calls them to walk according to the calling which they have received. They are called to be believers — it is then not too much to ask that they behave themselves as believers. It is only logical to do so. This is really the heart of the application of the gospel! Do what the gospel requires! Who sins unknowingly today? People know the way — it is only a question whether or not they will walk the way they profess.

Call to Christian Unity

The way in which the members of the church of Christ must walk has been spoken of in virtually every New Testament book. Here the Apostle sums up some of the things which are necessary for any believer. There must be a spirit of lowliness and meekness. There must be

longsuffering, forbearing one another in love. They must do
everything to keep the unity of the Spirit in the bond of
peace. Many will then go into an explanation of each of
these terms. This is permissible, but there are many other
terms which he uses in the other epistles. One can go into
these various terms and then forget what they are used for!
These are the things which must be observed to gain the
unity and peace of the church. One has to remember that in
the church at Ephesus, Jew and gentile were brought
together. Now all the haughtiness which characterized the
Jew in relation to others must be abolished! Otherwise there
will be no peace, and surely, no unity! Besides, the church,
by itself, is made up of all kinds of people. Here rich
and poor meet — the wise and simple sit at the same table.
Everyone, at all times, must observe the various virtues
he has mentioned to further the cause of peace and to
promote unity.

What Unites?

As I have mentioned in a previous Lesson in this series,
the one, holy, catholic church is an article of faith. There is
a unity and the members must seek the unity of the church.
So the Apostle speaks of this matter in this chapter. There is
one body — the church. There are not many churches nor
two, there is only one. Christ, of course, has only one body.
This is difficult to understand especially in our day when
the number of denominations in our country exceeds 250!
Many are loath to speak of the true church but would
rather work with a different concept of the church. One of
the churches in the Netherlands (by no means a splinter
group) speaks boldly of the address of the church! Many
find this far too exclusive. If the church has no *address* it
will be difficult to speak of the true and false church. Then
it doesn't make much difference where you go to church.
Then the sacraments have no address either. Then the Lord's

Supper can be celebrated at a retreat! If the church has no address, no one will be able to say much about the church. This is some of the confusion of today.

There is, therefore, only one body. There is also but one Spirit. Of course. The call of the gospel has come to these Ephesians and the Spirit of God applied that call, or gave the inner call. But, this was one call. Therein is their hope made complete because that call was the earnest of their inheritance. They have thereby been set on the road that leads to glory. There is only one Lord; there is only one faith; there is only one baptism. Anyone who would dare to claim that there is more than one Lord would be guilty of idolatry. There is but one way to be bound to that Lord — by faith. There is only that faith which has been wrought in the heart by the Spirit through the word. There is only one baptism. He mentions baptism because that is the sacrament whereby the people are brought into the fellowship of the church. It is that sacrament which symbolizes the washing away of sin through the blood of Christ and which symbolizes the union with Him and His body. There is also only one God, one Father. He is the one of Whom and through Whom and unto Whom are all things. Seeing there are only one Lord, only one God and Father, only one Spirit, one hope, one faith, and one call — how can there be more than one church? No, the unity of the church; though an article of faith, is a fact. Everything must be done to reveal and keep that unity. Not by means of a false ecumenicity, but by the true ecumenicity shown us in the Scriptures. God's people should do all in their power to bring together those who belong together, and should clearly brand as false church those who do not believe the teachings of Scripture. Our Confessions show us the way to do this.

An Individual Gift

In the unity of the church lies its strength. That unity must be displayed before men. However, the individual members of the church are by no means all alike. Each one has received different gifts from his Lord to be used for the benefit of the church. Out of this diversity of gifts the unity of the church comes to expression. This is the theme Paul stresses in Corinthians when he speaks of all the members of the human body having different functions (gifts) and all of them together forming one body. So it is in the church.

Given By the Ascended Christ

That the gifts which each individual believer has have come from the Lord Himself is made clear in the following verses. Paul refers to Psalm 68:18. This text deals with the ascension of Christ. He now tells the Ephesian church that through this ascension they have received so much. When He ascended, He came with the spoils of His victory. He has an abundance of gifts to bestow. Now this fact, He ascended, means that He must also have descended before this. Why should that be so? It is not true that anyone who ascends must first have descended? But this is true concerning the Christ because He had been above before, which was His natural station. Through His ascension He has filled all things with the multitude of His gifts and favor.

Gifts of Church Offices

Christ is the Source of all the spiritual gifts which have been bestowed on the individual believer. He also gives His gifts to the entire church. Some of these he now mentions. He gave some to be apostles, some prophets, some evangelists, and some pastors and teachers. The emphasis lies on the fact that these are gifts of Christ. The apostles were found only in the early church. The prophets too, through whom new revelations came. Evangelists will always be in the church as well as pastors and teachers. Seeing they are His gifts, the church must acknowledge them as such — he who rejects you rejects me!

Purpose of the Gifts

Paul now shows that the purpose of the gifts which He has given the church is to equip the membership of the church to reach its full potential so that each one is used for the perfecting and building up of the body of Christ, the church. This is, of course, the stimulation of the office of all believers. This is, and always has been necessary in the life of the church. Just so no one concludes that the church here below is ever able to do without the special gifts of Christ — the offices of which Paul has spoken. Nor may we conclude that that is the only purpose of the special offices, i.e., to enliven the offices of all believers. There is more! Christ wants His church fed! He wants His church led!

A Unity of Faith and Knowing Christ

Where a unity of the body is obtained there growth will also be found. On the other hand, where there is no unity, there can be no growth. If the church gratefully accepts the gifts the ascended Christ bestows upon it and finds itself equipped to the task to which the church is called, it will attain to a unity of faith and grow in the knowledge of the Son of God and become a full-grown, a mature man in Christ. Christians will not remain babes in Christ. Maturity must come. The writer to the Hebrews (Ch. 5, 6) urges his people to strive for the same goal. So only will they be strong in the faith. Then they will not always and forever have to go back to the elementary things, but will be able to press on to perfection. The author even speaks of attaining unto the measure of the stature of the fullness of Christ. No, we will not reach that goal here, but we should strive for it.

This growth in the faith is necessary for the unity of the church. There are examples enough in the New Testament of those who knew the way, and then were led astray like unstable children. Even one of the apostles, Peter, does not escape this evil. How often it is seen today that a congregation is instructed in the right way for several years, and another minister comes, and in a few years everything is turned upside down. How can people be so fickle? The antidote? Speak the truth! Let your yea be yea and your nay nay! How little of this is found today. But, let truth also be spoken in love. The truth separated from love is of no value. Only when we follow our Lord in His manner of living will we in all things grow up into Him. So we become like Him. So we begin to measure up to the stature of the fullness of Christ. You could depend on Him! He spoke the truth and did so in love.

A Growing Body

Coming to the conclusion of this section, the Apostle emphasizes the intimate relationship between Christ and the church. As so often in this epistle, he refers to Christ as the Head of the body. Here he means it in a strictly organic sense. That body is so beautifully "put together," it is a marvel. That is due to the fact that the head supplies all the things necessary for the proper functioning of every part of the body. Then each part of the body, doing that which is required of it, will help the whole body grow and answer to its purpose. To separate the body from its Head would be fatal and to separate any part of the body from the rest brings illness. Only as a harmonious whole can the body prosper and receive His blessing upon it.

Questions for discussion:
1. How must we seek the unity of the church? What is ecumenism? Is it proper?
2. What should be our first concern in seeking closer relations with other churches?
3. Is there only one baptism? Is there no difference between the baptism of Baptists and of Reformed?
4. How many offices are there in the church? May there be more or less?
5. What is meant by the office of all believers? This matter was not stressed prior to the Reformation and the great Reformation restored its recognition. Is there a danger today that we make too much of it?
6. How can you recognize the true church?

Lesson 9

The Contrast Between the Believer's and Unbeliever's Life

Ephesians 4:17-24

The church of Jesus Christ will somehow display a unity in the midst of a hostile world. We often despair of such a unity, but it is a fact despite the fact that there are all manner of branches of that one church of Christ. The Bible speaks of that unity often and there must be a display of it so that the world may also know the work which Christ Jesus has come to do.

Living the Faith

Now, therefore, i.e., because of all that has gone before, (Paul will emphasize, not only his own view of the matter, but he speaks in the name of his Lord) believers are to seek that unity of which he spoke by their manner of life. The believer must indeed believe that which is straight, which is true, which is *ortho*-dox, but that true belief must be accompanied by a life which is in tune with the doctrines believed. Therefore they are not to live as the gentiles. But, were these not gentiles to whom he is writing? He uses the term "gentiles" in two different senses. All those who were not Jews were gentiles and therefore these people in Ephesus, to whom he was writing, were indeed gentiles. However, one may also use the term in a different way to indicate those who are ungodly or uncivilized. It is in the latter manner that he uses the term here. The people Paul addresses have heard and believed the gospel, they were converted, they belong to Christ and consequently to His church, therefore they may no longer live as though nothing had taken place in their lives. They must walk in conformity to the faith they profess. How often this teaching is found in the Apostolic writings! It is one thing to profess the faith which has been proclaimed — it is a different matter to walk according to that rule.

Futility of Pagan Life

But, the readers of this epistle will certainly realize that the way of life which the Apostle has shown them is the only logical way. One who professes the true faith and then walks as the gentiles, is a living lie! The gentiles walk in the vanity, or futility, of their minds. They expect much of this world and this life, but it is vain and futile. It is disappointing. Nothing is adequately rewarded. In contrast, the life of the believer is rewarded far above anything he would ever be able to expect. *The Lord pays well!* It is also the only logical and consistent way of life. It is really a sad commentary on the believer's way of life that the Apostle must emphasize this matter so strongly. It ought to be a matter of course! In gratitude he ought to live a God glorifying life.

Ignorance of Unbelief

To make it even clearer why the believer is not to live as his unbelieving neighbors do, the Apostle gives a characterization of the life of the unbelievers. They are darkened in their understanding. That is, the unbelieving world which thinks that it has all wisdom and is therefore able to get along very well without God. Paul says their minds are dark — they live in intellectual gloom! They always were darkened in their minds and still are. The reasoning of the unbeliever has been affected by sin. This is a part of total depravity. He has spoken before of the fact that these Ephesian Christians had once been alienated from the commonwealth of Israel etc. Now he says of the gentiles around them that they are alienated from the life of God! That is much worse. Why is it so much worse for those who are now still gentiles? Because the gospel has come to Ephesus and they have, in their ignorance, spurned that gospel. Then it hardens. The gospel leaves no one the same. It is either a savor of life to life or it is a savor of death to death. Consciously these people had hardened themselves against the gospel. They consciously rejected it. These are now alienated from the life of God and have no part in the blessings given through Jesus Christ!

Moral Degeneracy

When this hardening occurs, it does not only affect the relationship to God and the gospel, no, it corrupts all relationships! This must never be lost from sight. Often the unbeliever is a "nice" person. Those who have hardened themselves become past feeling, they become calloused. Then they are basically not even "nice people" anymore. When people are beyond feeling they no longer realize their duties to fellow men. It is so strange that they then give themselves up to all uncleanness, i.e., on the surface. Why does this happen? When one consciously turns against the gospel of Jesus Christ and rejects it, he descends from that which is truly human to the animal level. Christ has come to fulfill, to complete the law of God. Only when men walk according to the law their God has given them will they attain to their true humanity. Therefore, whenever someone turns his back on the gospel he dehumanizes himself and gives himself to all manner of lewdness and covets iniquity.

Christ's Pupils

Having described the nature of the life of such gentiles, the Apostle warns believers not to imitate this kind of life.

Not only so, he shows them that the very opposite way of life has been taught them. They have "learned Christ". By this he means that they have not only learned about the Christ of God, but that they have learned to know *Him*! They have not only learned Him, but they are bound to Him. The acquaintance with Jesus Christ, and, what is far more, the implanting into Jesus Christ prohibits the kind of life the gentiles live. They have learned to know Christ so that they realize that He demands a life of devotion to Himself and a life which is unspotted by the sin of this world. They have learned to know Him as the One who leads to an essentially different outlook on life and goal in life. If they have learned to know Him they will flee from the kind of life they see the gentile living.

The things he is here contrasting ought to be clear to everyone who has heard the gospel of Jesus Christ. They have heard the word, have they not?

They have heard that truth is in Jesus, have they not? He (Christ) makes Himself known as the truth. Not only does He speak the truth — He is the truth! All the truths which are important to life are found in Him. Only He is able to make known the depth of man's sin. Of course, He is the only One who has made known the need and the nature of salvation. He too makes known to man the life of gratitude which he is to live before his God. Now, these are the essentials of knowledge. These are the things one must know both to live and die happily. The gentiles do not have the knowledge of any of these things. What is then the result? They give themselves up to all manner of sin and finally drown in their misery.

A Converted Life

Seeing these Ephesian Christians have been taught to know Christ and to know that truth is in Him alone, they must break with their former manner of life. They knew

what the Apostle had been speaking about. They knew
from experience. Their former life was like the unbelievers
around them at the present time. But, they have been
delivered from the bondage of that kind of life which those
who practice it call freedom. They must realize that the
salvation which they now embrace demands a complete
turnabout of all of life. It is not only a religion of the mouth
but of both word and deed. The whole outlook on life has
been radically changed for those who believe in Jesus.

A Process of Putting Off the Old
   The Apostle now uses terminology which he uses more
often to show them how complete this change is to be.
First of all, they must put off the old man. By this old man
he means the former way of life, the life which was
steeped in sin. Of course, basically they had put off the
old man when they believed on Jesus Christ — when they
had come to conversion. Then why this emphasis now?
This is a very important passage to show us that
everything is not completed when we have come to
conversion. This is one of the errors which is commonly
found today. Let a person confess that he believes on the
Christ of God and he has arrived! You can now go on to
the next one! This kind of theology Paul condemns.
Although something great has taken place when the eyes
are opened and the Savior is acknowledged, there is still a
long road ahead. One has to keep on putting off the old
man — that which entices to sin. The believer is faced
with the temptations to sin every day. Their former
manner of life may not be lived anymore — but the
temptation is there to do so. It is indeed one act of God
whereby the believer has been brought from death to life,
but for the believer himself there is a process whereby he
becomes more Christ-like.

Put On The New

The believer is, however, not only called to put off the old man but he is also admonished to put on the new man. Christianity is not only negative (it is that too) but it also has a very definite positive aspect.

The old man was the product. of sin; the new man comes out of regeneration. A new life has been created. This has to be evident in the life of him who professes to believe on Jesus as his Lord and Savior. The redeemed man must die to the old and be made alive to the new. He must turn from sin and seek holiness. He must learn to hate sin and love righteousness. He must flee the chaos of lawlessness and must rejoice in the law of God. He has indeed become a new creature!

In these verses the Apostle has taught the people in Ephesus, and thereby the church of all subsequent ages, the true balance which must characterize the life of those who have been redeemed by the blood of Christ. They must believe and work; they are faced with do's and don'ts; there is both the negative and the positive. Those who live according to the teaching of the Scriptures are not going to fall into the extremes which are so often seen. The Bible is to be our guide for all of life. It shows us the way of salvation and also teaches us how we are to live. When one tampers with the Bible he is undermining the faith and life of the people of God!

Questions for discussion:

1. Paul judges the understanding of believers to be far superior to that of unbelievers. How does the modern world judge this?
2. How does the process of hardening proceed?
3. Do you think that there are people who would like to stop with justification and forget about sanctification?
4. How have we learned to know Christ? Is it important how we learn to know Him? Are there some who have or are learning to know Him in the wrong way?
5. Is the believer still totally depraved?
6. Do we usually emphasize either the negative or the positive in our Christian life at the expense of the other? How can we keep our spiritual balance?

Specific Admonitions to the Ephesians

Ephesians 4:25-32

In the preceding paragraph the author has spoken of the antithesis between believer and unbeliever in his mode of life. He presented the principles on which a believing life is to be built. Now he is going from the general to the particular, he will become very practical in his teaching.

Stop Lying

Because of the things he has taught them in the previous paragraph, they will be able to understand the things he will now teach them. As they had been admonished to put off the old man of sin, so must they also put off the speaking of lies. This seems to be so elementary that one might wonder why the Apostle makes a point of mentioning this — and making it first in a series of admonitions. The law of God also forbids the speaking of falsehood (ninth commandment), because this is such a common sin. All sins fall under the moral law of God and of the six commandments dealing with our relationship to our fellow-man, one has to be devoted to this particular evil. Those who have come to believe the gospel and have given themselves wholly to it are to refrain from speaking falsehood. Instead, they are to speak the truth each one with his neighbor: for we are members one of another. To speak the lie is to break the brotherhood. Such practices make it impossible for the one to have true fellowship with the other. The lie destroys the church! The lie destroys

friendship! The lie destroys the family! In the words of
Jesus: Our yes must be yes and our no must be no. This
sounds so simple, but it is one of the most profound of all
His recorded statements and it is one which is violated more
often than almost any other. That one is not able to depend
on the word of the unbeliever might be expected; but the
unbeliever often puts the believer to shame in this area of
life. And, when you cannot depend on someone's word, all
relationships with him are broken.

Righteous Anger

   The place of anger in the life of any human being and
especially in the life of a Christian is an important matter
for anyone to consider. There is much anger displayed every
day. There is anger displayed by believers too. Is this
proper? Most of the time it is not because it is an evidence
of the presence of the old man of sin. But, it is unscriptural
to say that all anger is sin. God is angry with the wicked
every day. Our Lord was angry at times when He was here
on earth. It would be well if believers today would be filled
with righteous anger more often! When a worldly view of
love is emphasized in the church, there is no longer anger
against sin! The sinful deeds of men and the falsehoods
spoken under the guise of the gospel ought to fill our hearts
with anger. But, care must be taken that it is not a sinful
anger — in other words, there is an anger which is not
sinful. Nor, adds the Apostle, may we let the day come to
an end while we are still angry. What does he mean by this?
We may indeed be angry with the sinful deeds of others.
However, before the day has come to a close, we must be
reconciled. If anger is allowed to continue it will destroy the
person who harbors it, and that too will destroy the
fellowship of believers. I believe that the Apostle is here
emphasizing the need for *mutual discipline*. Be angry with
your brother when he goes contrary to the will of God!

Then see to it that this offense is removed the same day! This will make for a *healthy* relationship among believers. If this pattern of life is not followed, the devil will be the victor. The anger may have been righteous, but if the matter is not settled by means of confession and forgiveness, the devil has won the day. Righteous anger when not soon removed leads to a hardening and it soon becomes unrighteous!

Don't Steal, but Work

If the sin of bearing false witness is still common to the present day, surely the sin mentioned in verse 28 is not common (?). Paul tells those who are stealing not to continue in this error. This was a common sin. Those who do not speak the truth have already laid the groundwork for stealing another's goods. It was common in the heathen world of that day as it is in the heathen world of today. But, believers of every age better examine themselves too. Instead of stealing he should labor with his hands. He should engage in honest toil because such toil will be rewarded and he will then have sufficient to give to those who are not able to work. Paul's work ethic is mentioned in many of his letters. He himself worked day and night, and he does not approve of anyone not doing an honest day's work if he is able. Poverty is no blessing! It should be avoided and everything should be done to uproot it. By being diligent in his work a man will have more than enough for himself. Woe to those who do not alleviate the need of others!

No Foul Language

No one can deny that the Apostle is dealing with practical things and that he is specific in his admonitions. Believers' words must be true (vs. 25) but even more is required. The tongue is a very dangerous member of our bodies as well as

a very important member. It must speak the truth and it
may not speak that which is filthy! Dirty talk is one of the
devil's devices which he uses to corrupt men in the
unbelieving world and even the believers are not immune to
its temptation. The lie leads to all manner of sin... to
stealing etc. Filthy speech leads to many other sins, all of
these sins destroy the brotherhood! How dare men speak
filth with the same tongue which is used to pray to their
God!

Constructive Talk

As he spoke of these things in the previous paragraph and
in the first verses of this present paragraph, so he does here.
It is not only a matter of "Don't do this"! He also
emphasizes the positive. They must not engage in filthy talk
but they are to use their speech organs for a better purpose.
They must use their speech to build up their fellow believer
in the faith. This is not to be done in a very unrealistic way,
but "as the need may be". Then you have to know the
need! Speak so that it fits the situation! In this way your
speech will be a blessing to those who hear it. Corrupt
speech breaks down the fellowship of believers; godly
speech builds it up.

Don't Grieve the Holy Spirit

The things of which Paul has spoken ought to be
"natural" for the Ephesian Christians. Not only have they
believed in Jesus Christ unto redemption, they have, of
course, also received the Holy Spirit when they believed.
The Spirit of God dwells within
the believer to make him ever more holy. If such a person,
in whom the Spirit resides, does the works of the world, he
grieves the Spirit of God. The Spirit seeks his welfare now
and for eternity, and he goes contrary to it if he sins as the
unbeliever. Those who commit these sins are, therefore,

working against their own welfare. The gift of the Spirit to them was the down payment of their full salvation. In Him they are sealed till the day of redemption.

Sins to Be Discarded

In the conclusion of this section the Apostle mentions various sins, mostly of the tongue, or at least beginning there. Readers must be on the alert that they do not fall into the trap laid by the evil one by means of these sins. False speaking will lead to bitterness. This does not remain a sin of the tongue but ruins the heart and mind. Wrath and anger, too, consume those who practice these things. Clamor and railing go even beyond the former. They become loud protest and accusation against the fellow man. When these various steps have been taken they will lead to malice, i.e., the spirit which seeks the ruin of the opponent. The one sin begets the other, and each one is more evil than the one before. Now all these things must be put away from you, says Paul. There is no place in the life and conduct of the one who professes the name of Jesus Christ for such things as he has mentioned. Those who make themselves guilty of these sins have raised a real question as to the sincerity of their profession. Besides, they will be stumbling blocks to others.

Christian Virtues

As he has done before, so now the author reminds readers of the positive goals to which they are called as well as of the spurning of vices which they find in the unbelieving world around them. If the heart of man is desperately evil, then keep it tightly closed? No. If the tongue is capable of all these evils mentioned, then never speak again? No. God's gifts have been given to be used and not to be buried. Therefore, instead of all the evils mentioned, believers are to be kind one to another. All the things Paul mentions in the last verse of this chapter are, of course, to be done from the heart. Everyone knows what kindness is. This, they must practice, and it must be like the kindness God has shown to them. They are to be tenderhearted. They must be compassionate. The nature of the church demands that when one suffers all suffer and when one is glad all rejoice with him. This requires a compassionate heart. That is a heart which enters into the feelings of others. This is the essence of love.

One more item is mentioned — that they are to forgive one another as God also in Christ forgave them. This same note is sounded in the prayer our Lord taught us. "Forgive us ... as we forgive." To do this is difficult, in fact, impossible for those who have not been forgiven. But, the ten thousand talents which have been forgiven us are not to be compared to the hundred pence which we are asked to forgive. Yet, men find forgiving very difficult. How is this possible! Or have such people never tasted the forgiving love of God? To be forgiven we must repent. Those who find it difficult to forgive their fellow man also find it very difficult to repent of their own sins. It is the pride of the human hearts which makes it almost impossible to live according to the Apostle's injunction and thus makes it so difficult for them to be members of the church of Christ!

Questions for discussion:

1. Do you know many people you can really depend on? Will they speak the truth regardless of consequences?

2. Is it considered "nice" to be angry at something? Should we be angry or should love cover all things? What do you think of the statement heard almost daily: We must hate sin but love the sinner? Is this statement found in the Bible?

3. How far must we go in giving to the needs of others? Can we also do a real disservice to some by helping them out?

4. Is all spiritual talk edifying? What do you think of those who say "Praise the Lord" ten times in a ten minute conversation?

5. How do we get rid of such evils as are spoken of in verse 31?

6. May we ever sit in judgment on the spiritual life of another? Must we do so at times? Why is it important to understand this correctly?

Imitators of God

Ephesians 5:1-14

Some believe that the first two verses of chapter 5 belong with the material which has been treated in the previous chapter. However, it fits just as well with the thought the Apostle develops in the verses 3 to 14 of chapter 5.
He will speak of the manner of life to which believers are called in distinction from unbelievers. Therefore let them imitate God!

To say that we cannot imitate God because He is elevated far above us is to miss the meaning of the words which Paul is addressing to these Christians in Ephesus. He would not tell them to do the impossible and then cause a whole way of life to be dependent upon it. Of course we must imitate God. As a child imitates his father so must the believer imitate His God. He is His child! He will not be able to do the things God does — neither can a child do the things his father does. Still, he imitates him. That is the calling of believers, as beloved children, to imitate God.

Walk in Love

The manner of our imitating God is found in the next verse: Walk in love. So we imitate God. Our whole manner of life must be characterized by love, i.e., the kind of love Christ manifested to us. This is true love and it is the kind which is approved of God. God showed His love to us in Christ and Christ has shown His love to us in our redemption. He gave Himself up for us, an offering and a sacrifice to God as a fragrant aroma. His love to us was sacrificial! That is the pattern for our love! This is well-pleasing to God as a sweet fragrance.

This manner of life must be well understood by those who are members of the body of Christ. They must realize that their salvation is indeed dependent on their belief, but this belief must give rise to a life which is in accordance with the will of God. Throughout the history of the church there has been the danger that men would stress true beliefs even at the expense of a true life-style. Paul warns his people concerning this error. They are living in a world which not only ridicules the cross, they are also living in a world where the fumes of Satan's breath are in evidence wherever they turn. Immorality fills this world. All the talk of the present day that we are free from the law is denied by Paul and he shows the people of his day how dangerous it is to minimize but one of God's commandments. Fornication and uncleanness are the terms he uses to cover all the immorality that is found in the world of the Ephesians. These things are common in the world of sin, but they should be unheard of among believers. They are imitators of God! Covetousness or greed too is totally out of place in the life of a child of God. Redemption does not only save from eternal damnation, it also changes every aspect of life in the here and now. They are saints!

Their minds should not have place for filthiness of thought which will result in filthy language or deed. Their minds are to be pure, and if the thought is pure, the language and deed will also be pure. Their speech must not be the speech of fools. This is empty speech which enriches no one. They must not make themselves guilty of language which has double meaning because such talk is not fitting for believers. Language is a good gift and must be used as such. Speech is a wonderful gift of God and must be used for the giving of thanks. Then the believer shows that "his mouth, too, has been redeemed" and that he is sensitive to the demands of the third, seventh and ninth commandments.

Needed Warning — Exclusion from Christ's Kingdom

Those who do not believe on the Lord Jesus Christ have no inheritance in the kingdom of Christ and God. Neither do those who are fornicators or unclean persons or covetous men who are idolaters! So important is the walk of life to which the believer is called. It must be emphasized that the Apostle always makes a distinction between falling into sin or living in it. Therefore, those who live an adulterous life, a life of uncleanness, have no part in the kingdom of Christ. The covetous man, or the greedy man, is here identified with idolaters. Greed leads to idolatry. They serve Mammon rather than God! For such there is no place in His kingdom! When will the church stop compromising on these things? You surely know it to be true, says the Apostle! Let no one, therefore, deceive you with empty words. Anyone who teaches that believers need not be concerned about these ethical matters is deceiving them. The wrath of God rests on the immoral acts of men and also rests on those who teach falsehoods.

Paul has bestowed a great deal of labor on the church at Ephesus and does not wish to see those labors to be of no effect. But, Christ has a far greater "investment" in this church. Surely, His labors may not be in vain! Therefore the Apostle tells believers not to be partakers with the unbelievers in a life which goes contrary to the demands of the Christ. Christ's demands are always in perfect harmony with the law which God gave so many centuries before. Paul warns this people so that they may not be led astray. Before the gospel came to Ephesus these people, to whom he is writing, were in darkness and did the works of darkness just as the others. However, when the gospel came and the Spirit applied the Word to their hearts, they were changed. They became "light in the Lord." Is it, then, not logical that they should now walk as children of the light? It is a beautiful expression which he uses, i.e., they are children, or the offspring, of light. They must now be true to their new nature and so walk before Him. It is very easy for them to know whether or not they are walking as children of light. The fruit of the light is in all goodness and righteousness and truth. Their walk of life will not save them, but their walk of life will be the fruit of their salvation! Paul and James are often contrasted by men today as though they are in total disagreement with each other. Paul emphasizes faith and its content and James emphasizes the fruit of that faith. Each one has a different emphasis, but both speak of faith and both speak of the life as the result of faith. There is no disagreement but perfect harmony!

Fruit of the Spirit

How can a child of God be sure that he is really a child of God? This is the question which has plagued many people through the ages. Is there a possibility that He will speak directly to us to assure us of the fact that we belong to Him? Are there certain experiences which I must have before I can be sure? No, He has spoken in His Word and that is enough! When these Ephesian Christians believe the gospel as Paul has declared it to them and walk according to the demands of that gospel, they have the assurance of faith! This proves what is well-pleasing to the Lord! That is all they need.

No Fellowship With Works of Darkness

Once more Paul refers to the deeds of the unbelievers as he had spoken of them in the early part of this chapter. The believers must not have fellowship, must not partake, of these deeds. Really, they cannot have fellowship with these deeds because they are works of darkness while the believer is a child of light. Besides, they are unfruitful works while the believer's life must be fruitful. He is called to reprove these works of darkness. Yet, the things which the unbelievers do in secret — it is even a shame to speak of them, says Paul. If you cannot speak of them, how can you reprove them? Precisely in the way he had outlined in the previous verses.

By their walk, their godly walk, they will reprove the works of darkness. Men will be able to see the emptiness of the unbeliever's life in the light of the godly walk of believers. Here, as in so many places, Paul teaches the antithesis! There is no compromise possible between light and darkness; between the life of the believer and the unbeliever; between good and evil. The lines are drawn sharply! The gospel of Jesus Christ cannot and may not be tied to the mistaken notions of other religions!

Only when the lines are sharply drawn will the works of darkness be exposed for what it really is. Only the light which believers have and are is able to expose the evil. Whenever God's people compromise their beliefs, the gospel is obscured and the unbeliever is left in the dark. The true light of the gospel makes visible the true character of sin. For his own welfare the believer must walk according to the principles shown him in the Word of God, but also for the welfare of his fellowman. The child of God is doing no one a service by minimizing the sin of others... Only the light makes things manifest — let it then shine!

Rise and Shine

The words found in verse 14 are a quotation but we do not know the source of this quotation with any certainty. Many believe that the Apostle is quoting Isaiah 60:1, but it certainly is not a verbatim quotation. Nor is this of much importance. He quotes with approval and makes clear that it is the Word of God. That's all that is necessary to know. He is, by means of these words, calling to the unconverted to awake. But, he is also calling to those already converted but not living the consistent Christian life to awaken. The unbeliever is surely sound asleep, but the inconsistent believer is also slumbering. Let them awake out of their sleep and arise from the dead and Christ shall shine upon them. He will give them the true light and the true life, and He is the only Source of both! Let no one say: But they cannot awaken because God only is able to awaken them out of their sleep! Let no one say this — but many do! Then there are many parts of Scripture which become a riddle and we have set our own logic as the standard for the Bible! It is true, of course, that salvation is God's work from beginning to end. But, man is a responsible creature! He tells him: Believe! and that man better not have the audacity to say: I can't! He tells men to turn, and they are called to obey! So here too: Awake! ...and *arise from the dead*!

Let men realize that they are to be obedient to Him in their whole walk of life.

Questions for discussion:

1. How can we imitate God and how can we not do so?
2. How dangerous is immorality to our spiritual life? What does this have to say to us about marriage and divorce? As to literature and movies?
3. Is it dangerous to teach that the law is not for us? What do we stress most, right doctrine or right living? May we ever separate them?
4. How should we reprove those who sin? Are we guilty before God if we do not reprove sin?
5. What is the danger of saying: We cannot believe, God must give it to us? Can this also lead to "cheap" religion? Yet, it is true — we cannot believe all by ourselves. Whence comes that faith? But, is the impression often left He hasn't given me these things, therefore I am blameless?

Lesson 12

Living Wisely

Ephesians 5:15-21

This paragraph is very closely connected to the words found in the previous section. There the Apostle had urged his readers to imitate their God in their whole manner of life. To do this they must keep themselves from all immorality. Their manner of life must make it clear to all men that they are serving a new Master and that they have a different goal in life. In the present paragraph Paul gives further advice concerning specific aspects of the way of life which is approved of God and is in tune with their own confession.

Watch Your Step

They are to look carefully at their way of life. This is not an inconsequential matter. True, their profession must be true to the Word of God in every respect. But, their lives may not militate against their profession nor against the clear commandments He has given them. Let them, therefore, consider their walk of life carefully. This will be a witness to all those who are "watching" them. Their word of witness may not conflict with the life-style which everybody is able to see. To walk carefully is the wise manner of life. It agrees with their confession which is true. If they walk as those who have not embraced the gospel of Jesus Christ, they would live unwisely. In these words the Apostle puts the matter very mildly, but they are words which everyone will understand.

Seize the Opportunity

These readers are called to "redeem," or to buy up the

time or opportunities, because the days are evil. These words are very well-known but are often misunderstood. Are there many opportunities which must be bought up at any price if the days or times are evil? These evil days would seem to make these opportunities rare. And, that the days were evil in which these Ephesians were living is clear from the previous section. The Christian church had been placed in the midst of a hostile world — and that is still her place! She must now live in a manner which will reveal the depth of the iniquity of the unbelieving world. The church may not have the opportunity to *speak*, let her therefore *live* her confession! It is amazing what can be done in this way. Christians must use every opportunity, they must buy them up, because they are so scarce! Much can be done by the church of Christ if each member will use the God-given opportunities to bring honor to the name of Christ. The history of the Christian church contains many names of heroes of faith who used the opportunities given them in their time. We use only a small part of our intellectual capacity and that is also true concerning our stewardship of the spiritual capacities given us. How much some have accomplished! How little the majority accomplish! Redeem the time!

The things which Paul has mentioned ought to be so self-evident that everyone would be in complete agreement with his statements. However, that is not the case. These things must be taught again and again. Yet, it is certainly clear to all that his teaching here is the only wise course for a believer to follow. Paul now reiterates the things said in verse 15 but makes them somewhat stronger. Let Christians not walk as fools. Let them not be without understanding in the manner of life which they live. This would indeed be the case if they did not heed his admonition. That wrong walk of life is not only sinful, it is also foolish! Many may deny the presence of sin, but nobody wishes to appear foolish. To safeguard yourselves, understand what the will of the Lord is. He has spoken clearly to them. He has made known what manner of life is well-pleasing to Him, i.e., the life which naturally flows from a true confession. Let them live their faith and the questions will not be multiplied: May I do this? Why may I not do that? etc.

Not Drunk with Wine, but Filled with the Spirit

Paul now gives a very clear example of his teaching in the previous verse. They must not be drunken with wine but be filled with the Spirit. How often the New Testament refers to the misuse of wine! It was a problem then and it has been a problem through the ages. It is not true that the Bible forbids the use of wine, but it certainly gives clear warning against its misuse. Would it not have been better if the Bible had clearly forbidden its use? Then, however, we would be wiser than God. These readers of this epistle must realize that the evil one uses wine to anesthetize his victims. The days are evil for believers but they were also difficult for unbelievers. They then make misuse of wine to drown their life's sorrows. But, therein is riot, or uncontrolled living. That leads to the foolishness against which Paul has warned. It does not give joy or deliverance but increases the pain. Instead of being drunken with wine the Apostle urges them to be filled with the Spirit. This will bring the true joy of life; it will be in keeping with their profession of their faith in Christ; and it will be the pathway of life which is wise and not foolish. What a contrast — drunken with wine or filled with the Spirit! But, so great is the contrast between believer and unbeliever!

A Life of Song

The life of a believer is a life of song. The largest book of the Bible is the Psalter for Israel and for the church of all ages. Christianity is the religion of song. Other religions have nothing to sing about and consequently singing has a very inferior role in the lives of their devotees. The believer, whether of Old Testament times or of the New, has reason for song and his God has given him the inspired song book. In a measure we are even able to sing of the mighty deeds of redemption by means of the Psalms; however, hymns are necessary to do justice to our jubilation in Christ's coming and His resurrection, etc. When the Apostle here speaks of Psalms and hymns and spiritual songs, I do not believe that he is making sharp distinctions between them. He means that believers are to edify one another with such song as is approved. There were a few hymns already at that time as well as the Psalter. They are to engage in singing and making melody with their hearts to the Lord. Their life is to be a song! Their hearts overflow with joy and this seeks expression in song.

How different is the expression of joy on the part of the believer from that on the part of the unbeliever. The latter is drunken and may sing out in a drunken inebriation, while the believer sings the praise of his God. The believer does so consciously while the unbeliever doesn't know what he is doing. Those who make melody with their hearts to the Lord do not engage in "idle" songs or "ditties." The true church sings! It sings Psalms! It glorifies God and not the singer!

By means of the songs which the redeemed of the Lord sing, they bring thanks to their God. How often the Psalmist urges the people of his day to give thanks to God for all they have received out of His hand. In Psalm 103 he even instructs himself to give thanks. This giving of thanks can be done in different ways, but song is certainly one of the most prominent ways. The Apostle now encourages his readers to a life of gratitude. He does this in many places in his writings, but in this beautiful passage he does so in a very special way.

Thanks Always for All Things

Do they have reason to be grateful? Notice that the author proceeds on the assumption that God's people always have reason to give thanks. He simply is not able to conceive of a situation in which the Christian would not have reason to be grateful. Therefore he uses sweeping terms — "always" — "for all things." How is this possible? We must realize that he is not just writing words which have no meaning for the everyday life of a believer. He knows whereof he speaks, and, he is writing the Word of God. He himself is a prisoner in Rome at the time he is writing to the Ephesians that they must always be thankful for all things. Can he be thankful for the fact that he is in prison in chains? Not only is this possible for him, but he rejoices therein and gives expression to his feelings concerning these matters time and again in his writings. His Savior is in control of all things and He knows what He is doing! This man, Paul, is a marvel! He truly lives his confession. He shows a Christian optimism which has seldom been equaled. He does not come with "dry" teaching; he comes with the vibrant Word of God which these Ephesian (and other) Christians desperately need.

This thanks is to be expressed to God. This reveals the character of the approved songs too. In our songs we do not engage in subjective expressions, but God is the object of our praise and thanksgiving. Only in the name of our Lord Jesus Christ are we able to approach our God. The songs of praise must have the approval of Christ and so will they be received by the God to Whom they are sung. That which would praise man would naturally be contraband; that which would even praise our faith or prayer would be suspect! We are to bring our praise and thanks to Him from whom all blessings flow!

In Christ's Name

The praise of God and the thanks to God of which Paul has been speaking, though difficult to carry out, will, nevertheless, receive the approval of those who read these words. But, there is more. In the following paragraphs he is going to speak of the relationships which these Christians are to have toward their fellow men. Then there will be many more questions in their minds. He is, therefore, going to write a few words which will form a transition to the subjects with which he will deal in the following sections. He tells them that they are to subject themselves one to another. This is not desirable in the eyes of many. However, their Lord had spoken in the same vein. No one is to seek the first place, but meekness is required. This has also made Christianity odious to many. We must remember that Paul does not teach that one must always be subject to everyone. This becomes an absurdity! One will finally emerge above another. What does he teach? This meekness must be found in the fear of Christ. It is not to be meekness for meekness' sake, but for Christ's sake! The one must be willing to subject himself to others in reverence for Christ. This is the life and walk of wisdom!

Questions for discussion:

1. Are our opportunities for service to our God well used? Do we always see the opportunities?
2. Many do not care for the Christian manner of life because they believe it is too restrictive. How does this attitude reveal their foolishness?
3. Heresy has often entered the church through song. Does this apply to the words only or can even the music be harmful?
4. Do we need hymns in the New Testament church? Do we sing the Psalms enough? Is some of our hymnody too subjective? Explain.
5. Can we be thankful for everything? For sickness? For losses? Are we not taught to pray for the removal of "obstacles" in our lives?
6. Do some Christian groups have the wrong view of meekness? Does the teaching on meekness mean, e.g., that we would never insist on our rights? That we would never go to court?

Lesson 13

Christ and the Church: The Pattern for the Home

Ephesians 5:22-33

Wives and Husbands

This paragraph has received more unfavorable attention in our day than any other part of the Epistle to the Ephesians. Paul is dealing with a relationship which is undergoing great changes in our age. What is the proper relationship between husbands and wives? Our time prefers to look upon that relationship as one of equality, as two equals bound together by voluntary ties. This is the democratic ideal and gets away from the so-called antiquated view which is still found in certain places in human society today, but not in enlightened circles!

Paul begins this section in a way that jolts many today. He tells wives to be in subjection to their own husbands! He has been maligned as one who is a woman hater. Was he not unmarried? Is he speaking the language of his own day and is he not adopting the common views of his society? The answer to these and similar questions gets to the heart of the "problem." It is essentially a question of the view of Scripture one possesses. Is Paul giving his own view of these matters or is this paragraph also inspired by the Spirit of God? If one does not hold to the latter position, nothing in the Pauline writings is normative for the man of today. He does not only speak of this matter in this paragraph but he refers to it again and again in his various letters to churches and individuals. It is, therefore, a very important matter. It must be properly understood in order to have the proper view of the most basic of human relationships!

"Be Subject"

Wives are, therefore, to be subject to their husbands. Why? Because he is the wiser of the two? Because he always has the better judgment? Of course not! Why? Because God says so! Men may think themselves wiser than God and reverse His order, but they will pay the price! His Word stands. This *subjection* is the stumbling block for many. But, the Apostle makes it very clear in the following verses how the rule of the one and the subjection of the other are to be understood. Here he simply says that she is to be subject to her husband as unto the Lord. The husband is standing in the place of the Lord — he has received an *office*. He will be responsible to the Lord for the way he governs his house. Let the wife therefore not be blinded by all the inadequacies of her husband, but let her look on him as representing the Lord in her home.

The Husband Is Head

He emphasizes this relationship even more in verse 23. He says very clearly that the husband is the head of the wife! That is the reason she must be subject. This is the way in which the Creator has formed the first home. Adam was created first — then Eve. Some may not like this divine arrangement, but, who can argue that that is not the manner in which the Bible always presents the matter? To make it clear that this is not a relationship under which the one suffers hardship, Paul immediately adds: "as Christ also is the head of the church." If there would be a different relationship between Christ and the church than the one spoken of here, Christ would be dethroned and the church would be lost! So important is it, therefore, to see the husband-wife relationship in the proper light. The wife is not called to servile subjection, but natural subjection. Not as a slave, but in love. Christ is the Savior of the body, the church. He, though the head of the body, is seeking its welfare. If the church should seek a place equal to that of Christ, she would destroy herself! The church must be subject to Christ in order to obtain salvation. This is not a galling yoke, no, His commands are not grievous. So are the wives to be subject to their own husbands "in everything." This last phrase does not mean slavish subjection, regardless of what he may require, but, rather, subjection as the common pattern of life.

Husbands Commanded to Love

Husbands are commanded to love their wives! Can we love at command? Yes, and if a husband no longer loves his wife he is disobedient! This apostolic statement presupposes the Biblical view of love. Not as modernity would have it — involving only the emotions; but a love which is deep and involves the whole person. Husbands love your wives in that way. They are herein also to follow the pattern shown them by Christ. He loved the church! What kind of love was that? Sacrificial! He gave His life for her. That is the way husbands are to love their wives and it will then not be difficult for the wife to be subject to her husband!

The metaphor which the Apostle uses in this section cannot be pressed in all its various parts. This is true concerning the words we find in verses 26 and 27. The main point of the illustration may never be lost from sight, but all of the details cannot be applied to both Christ's relation to the church and the marriage relationship among men. Christ has given Himself for the church so that He might set her apart (sanctify), and that He might cleanse her "by the washing of water with the word." Without doubt a reference is here made to baptism. However, baptism in association with the Word! Let no one derive a faulty view of baptism from this verse, but let everyone see it in its context. By baptism He indeed cleanses, i.e., baptism is a symbol of this cleansing. However, that baptism never stands alone but is united to the word and in that way the cleansing *goes on*! It is a life-long process. In this way the Lord will finally present a church to Himself which has neither spot nor wrinkle, but is a glorious and *cleansed* church. The people of his day understood Paul when he referred to these things, especially the Jews among them. However, they must also have wondered at the language of the Apostle when he speaks as he does here. It was customary among the Jews that a bride would *prepare herself* for her wedding day. But, Paul says that Christ prepares His bride! The metaphor, therefore, is altered a little in these two verses, but that is common in the Paul-me writings. What illustration shall he choose which will cover both the divine and human relations? His emphasis here is on the fact that Christ cares for His church and sees to it that that church shall be holy and without blemish. Now, "even so ought husbands also to love their own wives as their own bodies." So close is the bond between Christ and His church and between husband and wife that he is able to say that the husband who so loves his wife — loves himself! Where do the duties lie — on the side of the wife or on that of her husband? On neither, or both, because it is a work of love!

Of course, no one hates his own flesh. (There are too many who conceitedly love it too much) Each person, — of course, seeks the welfare of his own body. Otherwise that body becomes sick and malfunctions. Therefore a person nourishes and cherishes it. Christ nourishes and cherishes His church. Seeing that we are members of His body we must emulate Him. We must, as husbands, bestow that loving care on our wives which Christ bestows on His church. Then our relationship to Christ is shown in clear light.

Beginning at the Creation — One Flesh

The Apostle now goes all the way back to the time of creation to show that the things he has been teaching concerning the true relationship of husbands and wives goes all the way back to the beginning. The command was there given that a man (and woman?) should leave father and mother and cling to his wife when they have been joined in marriage. Naturally, this was a command to future generations because Adam had no father or mother to leave. The emphasis falls on the unity of the two who have entered the marriage state. They shall become one flesh. They shall be one in mind and in heart (how shall two walk together except they be agreed?) but there shall also be a sexual union — a union of bodies. All of a man's attention must be focused on his wife. Even that close relation which he had to his father and mother may not stand in the way of his relationship to his wife. He must forsake the former to cling to the latter. This is the way marriage was intended to be from the beginning! This is the way marriage is renewed through our union with the Christ of God! Christian marriage is a symbol of the union of Christ and His church. Therefore a religiously mixed marriage is wrong! How can an unbelieving husband be a symbol of Christ? How can an unbelieving woman be the symbol of His church? Mixed marriage is, therefore, basically wrong — and it is not wrong, first of all, because it doesn't work!

A Mystery — Applied

"This mystery is great: but I speak in regard of Christ and of the church." This seems to be a strange statement in the middle of this discussion. We also have to be careful that we do not give a wrong or fanciful meaning to these words, as has often been done. In the first place, by the term *mystery* Paul always means that which had not been revealed before but now is revealed. He is here, I believe, emphasizing the same thing I emphasized earlier, viz., that the metaphor is insufficient to cover all of the various parts of the relationship of Christ and the church and of husband and wife. The marvelous love which Christ exhibited to His church cannot be equaled, but it is the goal for which we are to strive. Even though he is speaking regarding Christ and the church, nevertheless, husbands are to love their wives according to the pattern shown them by Christ. That love must be deep and it must be self-sacrificing. There must be no doubt that the man has this kind of a love for his wife. On the other side, the wife must see to it that she fears or has respect for her husband. This latter, of course, does not rule out the love she must have for him, nor could his love for her rule out the respect he must have for his wife.

Wherever these rules of marriage are not recognized or obeyed, marriage fails to achieve its purpose. We must again get back to the Biblical view of the true marriage bond, or our problems will multiply in this important area of life. The place of the one is not devalued for the sake of the other, as is so often assumed today. Only when we follow the teachings of Scripture will we have the fullness of life.

Questions for discussion:

1. Does this paragraph in Ephesians have anything to say concerning the matter of Women in Office? If so, what does it teach concerning it?

2. What does the "headship" of the husband mean? Is there the danger that this shall become a dictatorship?

3. What is wrong with coming to a decision together, as husband and wife, after full discussion? Do you think this paragraph forbids this?

4. Can we love at command? What counsel would you give someone who states that he or she simply no longer loves the other party in the marriage relationship?

5. Do mixed marriages sometimes "work." Does this mean that it isn't always wrong?

6. The Bible deals with the marriage relationship in many places. Why have we had many committees to study what would be proper guidelines for marriage? Why did we need many committees to study the matter of divorce?

Lesson 14

Of Children and Slaves

Ephesians 6:1-9

At the beginning of this last chapter the writer singles out certain groups in the church at Ephesus for whom he has a special word. This implies, of course, that these (children, slaves, masters) were in the church service where this apostolic letter was read. He often singles out particular groups in the churches to which he writes. *All* the members of the church were expected to be present when the great event of receiving a letter of Paul occurred. So it ought to be throughout time and throughout the church. The gospel speaks to each one and no one has a right to be absent where the Spirit of God speaks.

"Children Obey Your Parents in the Lord"

Paul addresses the children with a command which is derived from the fifth commandment and he quotes that commandment in the second verse. A child is to be obedient to its parents. This is the teaching of nature and all of life. The child may not be in the position in which it commands! The child is in need of being led and of being instructed. It must therefore listen to those who are older and wiser. But, the children of believers are not only taught by nature, they are especially taught by the Word of God. They must not obey because no other behavior is possible for them, but they must obey willingly and gladly "in the Lord." He requires it and what He requires is right.

In the second verse the Apostle quotes the first part of the fifth commandment. This commandment does not speak first of all of obeying father and mother, but of honoring them. This is an important distinction. At no time does the child arrive at the age when he is not to honor his parents, but the time for obeying them is limited. Honoring them is, therefore, of a more fundamental nature. It will include the obedience which is required in the early years of life. By bringing the proper honor the child gives evidence of a true love for his parents. And... , that is the heart of the law! Obedience may be because of fear of the consequence of disobedience, etc., but honor reveals love and devotion.

"Commandment with Promise"

This is the first commandment with promise, says Paul. Is that entirely correct? Does not the second commandment already include a promise that He will show loving kindness to thousands of those who love Him and keep His commandments? Different explanations have been given of this seeming error. We should remember that the promise found in the second commandment is general in nature and could have been attached to any of the ten commandments. Secondly, he is not necessarily using the term "first" in a numerical sense. Here a promise is attached to a specific commandment which has meaning for the keeping of this commandment only.

The promise is now quoted: that it may be well with thee, and thou mayest live long on the earth. However, this promise has also given difficulty to many. It surely is not true that every obedient child will live to a ripe old age? Would that not be the natural meaning of the wording of this promise? In dealing with the ten commandments it certainly becomes evident to everyone that a key sin is mentioned but that each one of these commandments is much broader in scope than the particular sin which is mentioned. The Heidelberg Catechism makes this very clear in its treatment of each one of the commandments of the Decalogue. It then becomes clear that the fifth commandment does not only deal with the relationship of parent-child, but also of government-governed, of employer-employee etc. When one considers how far this commandment reaches, the promise included in this commandment becomes clear. If this commandment is transgressed in all the various relationships of life, there would be utter chaos! This would make life impossible. Only where there is a well-ordered life, in obedience to this commandment, can *a people* look for a lengthy life in the land which the Lord gives to them. A home, a society, a government can endure only where this commandment is honored!

Fathers' God-Given Trust

The fifth commandment speaks to parents as well as to children. It is true that the children are to obey, but the parents must also insist on this obedience and make it as easy as possible for the child to be obedient. The author addresses the fathers in particular. They are the ones who are responsible for maintaining the proper relationship in the home. The father is the "head" of the home. He is also the one who enforces discipline in the home. Paul makes it clear to fathers that they do not have all the rights and the children all the duties. The child has duties but he also has rights. The fathers must not provoke their children to wrath. That is a real danger! This can be done by physical means or mental or even spiritual means. Parents sometimes deprive their children of all hope and of the joy of life. This is an abuse of the position their God has given to them as fathers. Instead, they must nurture them in the chastening and admonition of the Lord. To be a father is a tremendously responsible task. It is not enough that a father provide food and clothing and other such necessities, but he must nurture them, bring them up, teach them the things of the Lord. The eternal welfare of his children must certainly be of as great concern to a father as their material welfare. Who is sufficient unto these things? When a father is true to his calling as a father, he will make it much easier for the child to obey the fifth commandment. This will insure God's blessing on both. This will also insure a church made up of strong families who bow before the Word of God.

Duty of Christian Slaves

The second specific group which the Apostle addresses are the servants and masters within the church. Many have been disappointed because this author does not condemn slavery and do his utmost to uproot it. Isn't slavery totally inconsistent with Christianity? Of course! However, the approach which Paul takes to this problem is not revolutionary. He brings up the subject in almost all of his epistles and the message is always the same: servants (or slaves) be satisfied with your lot in life; and masters, treat your servants well. We may, however, not lose sight of the fact that he is destroying the institution of slavery with the Word much more effectively than any revolutionary has ever done. If slaves and masters both heed the teachings he gives them, slavery will be destroyed from within, which is far more effective than attacking it from without. It must, therefore, also be observed that Paul never upholds slavery. The gospel has come into that particular social and economic setting and seeks to remold all of life from within.

Paul counsels the slaves to be obedient to those who are their masters according to the flesh. That is the proper place of slaves. If they do not render obedience, they have denied the relationship in which they stand to their masters. But, they must remember, these are only masters over the flesh, not over the spirit. It is well possible to find a slave who is much more free than his master. But, be obedient to masters because it has, for the present, pleased God to place them over you. Do so with fear and trembling. By these two terms he does not mean that they should grovel before their masters but that they should be conscientious in doing the tasks assigned to them and that they should be sincere in their attitude to their masters. They must bring service as though they are bringing it to the Christ Himself. Suddenly the master over their flesh has assumed the place of Christ. This teaching is important for them in doing their work properly.

Serving as Unto the Lord

This manner of bringing proper service is so important that he spends a few more verses on this same topic. They must not try to be well-pleasing to men while the heart isn't in it. They must work as servants of Christ, doing the will of God from the heart. This will become evident to all over a period of time. Only when they conduct themselves in this way will the masters, whether they be believers or unbelievers, have to come to the conclusion that these people have a different Source of life and a different goal than others. Again Paul says that they are to do service with a good will as unto the Lord, and not unto men. After all, they are rendering service to Christ regardless of the position in life He has given them. That they have this position of servants isn't so bad either, because their Lord assumed that same role voluntarily on their behalf. Must they all be rulers while their Lord became a servant? He also reminds them that the Lord will reward every good thing which they have done and it makes no difference whether they were bond or free when they did these good deeds. Here again the Apostle emphasizes the good-works of believers even though he has shown so clearly in the first chapters that salvation is of the Lord alone. Nevertheless, good works must come to light as fruits of the faith which has been instilled within them. This obedient faith brings forth fruits which the Lord rewards.

Duty of Christian Masters

The last word in this connection is addressed to the masters. There were some of these among the members of the church because the gospel had not only been preached to the down-and-outs. These masters must also show in their relation to their slaves that they have been changed by the gospel. Paul tells them to do the same things to them, meaning the slaves. He, of course, does not mean that these masters must be obedient to the slaves! No, but he has taught the slaves to seek the welfare of their masters in the work and manner of work they did; so must the masters now also seek the welfare of their slaves! They must also stop threatening their slaves. What defense would a slave have against such threatening? Their threatenings would be making misuse of the place they have in their particular society. They are believing masters and must therefore realize that they are also under the jurisdiction of Another. That One is their Master as well as the Master of their slaves. He is in heaven and is not a respecter of persons. In other words, before Him it makes no difference whether they are masters or slaves. He will demand His due from them both!

If these words which have been directed to both slaves and masters are taken to heart, slavery will not be able to exist beyond that generation! Because these words were not obeyed in many places the institution of slavery continued till modern times!

Questions for discussion:

1. What is the difference between honoring and obeying one's parents? Is this an important difference? Why?
2. How does the promise fit the fifth commandment?
3. How can parents provoke their children to anger? Is this child abuse?
4. Why doesn't the New Testament simply forbid slavery?
5. Do you agree that the Scripture's dealing with slavery would obliterate it in a short time?
6. Does the Bible teaching about the master-slave relationship have anything to say to us today concerning the employer-employee relationship?

Lesson 15

The Militant Church

Ephesians 6:10-13

Glorious things have been written about the church in the epistle to the Ephesians! The church is the fulfillment of the "mystery" which had never been revealed before. Jew and gentile, rich and poor, bond and free, learned and unlearned — they all meet together in the church. Paul has also spoken of the "dimensions" of the love of Christ which has been revealed in the church. This true church of Jesus Christ is the one outside of which is no salvation (Belgic Confession Art. 28). This church has been organized at Ephesus! The truth has been made known there. The members have tasted of the glorious salvation which Christ has brought. Is it all joy in the life of that church? Surely, God will guard that church. It shall stand to the last day. Even the gates of hell shall not prevail against the true church. However, that church will remain standing only if she recognizes her responsibility and strives valiantly. Those are the things of which the Apostle speaks in the last chapter of this epistle.

"Be strong in the Lord"

The members of this church are counseled to "be strong in the Lord, and in the strength of his might." They must realize at the outset that they will not be able to stand, far less conquer, in their own strength. Why not? For the simple reason that they have no strength in themselves! Let them be humble in accepting the gospel of Jesus Christ and let their humility continue in the exercise of their spiritual responsibility. This will become clearer in the following verses. But, the fact that they have no strength in themselves should not discourage them, because they are able to draw on a strength which is far superior to any they could have imagined. They are to be strong in the Lord! They must live close to Him and no evil shall befall them. Only in His power will they be able to do what is required. He has an inexhaustible supply of strength for them. He is the almighty One not only in creation and in providence, He is also the Almighty One for the salvation of His people. He has revealed to them that He is both able and willing to give aid to His people. They can look back at all the things He has done in the past for the help of His people. He led Israel out of Egypt; He gave Canaan into their hand; He slew kings for their sakes; He raised Jesus from the dead and exalted Him to His right hand. Let them believe in the Lord but let them also stand strong in Him! They will have to strengthen themselves in Him every day and every moment of their lives.

"Put on the Whole Armor of God"

To be able to stand strong in the Lord they will be required to put on the whole armor of God, which he explains later as to its various parts. Let it be clear immediately that it is an armor which He supplies. Also, that it is an armor which believers must put on. God supplies all the things necessary but it is not an evidence of faith to say that if He wishes, He will safeguard them. No, they have the responsibility of putting on this armor which He supplies. Only in this way will they be strong in the Lord and in the strength of His might.

Able to Stand

Let them be assured that they will be able to stand in the battle for their souls if they are faithful to the commands which he gives them. This may be difficult for them to grasp because they will have to face the wiles of the devil! Paul believes there is a personal devil. He believes there is that person of the most extreme evil who attacks the church and seeks to destroy it (Rev. 12). He is afraid of this power because he knows it is great and ruthless. Yet, the power of Jesus Christ is far greater than that of the devil. The Lord will finally vanquish him. But, they, the members of the church, must stand in the strength of the Lord! That is the only safe place.

"Wiles of the Devil"

Not only does he speak of the devil as their antagonist, but he reminds them of the "wiles" of the devil. He doesn't fight fairly. He uses deception. He uses ambush. He uses any methods available to him. He mixes truth and error. He even comes with the words of Scripture — as in the temptations of our Lord. He reveals himself as an angel of light, while he is the prince of darkness. The people at Ephesus and all who read this epistle must therefore be on their guard. The prayer "Lead us not into temptation" receives new urgency here. How shall they ever be able to stand against such a dreadful and ruthless power which also makes use of every means of deception? Humanly speaking, they will not be able to stand. But, God has supplied them with armor. That is all they need — but they need this desperately. No armor of man will do. Putting on the whole armor of God they will be able to stand, i.e., hold their ground. They will not be overcome by the evil one. The victory will ultimately belong to the Christ and to those who have placed their trust in Him.

A Spiritual Warfare

Now the Apostle informs his readers as to the nature of the battle in which they will be engaged. He says that the wrestling is not against flesh and blood. It is not against men or other physical creatures. If it were, it would be an equal match. Then they might find an armor which would satisfy. Men have often mistakenly thought their enemy to be other men. But, this is not the case. In the previous verse Paul has spoken of the wiles of the devil and he now explains more fully what kind of adversary the believers will meet. It is a spiritual conflict. The foe cannot be seen. The foe does not have the weaknesses which are common to men. He, or they, have tremendous power. He refers to them here as "principalities," "powers," "world rulers of this darkness," "spiritual hosts of wickedness in the heavenly places." This is a description of the host of the wicked fallen angels. These are the ones who dared to defy God and were cast out of the heavens. Believers are completely surrounded by these evil forces. They have no moment of truce. The tactics of this evil host change constantly but the goal always remains the same: ruin the work of God! It is difficult to fight this kind of a foe because it is an overwhelming host. It has superhuman power.

Controlling Powers

When the Apostle speaks of the world rulers of this darkness we see some of the means which they employ for the destruction of the faith of God's people. The evil one is in control of the false philosophies which fill this world. This is the darkness which even attacks the revelation of God! At the instigation of the evil one, men sit in judgment on the word of God itself. This darkness blinds men and leads them astray. It has slain its thousands throughout the history of the church. This darkness is not lifted as time progresses but becomes deeper. This darkness achieves its greatest triumph in the days of Antichrist. Believers must be on their guard that they are not misled by these world-rulers of this darkness. God allows them to rule in this realm for this time.

Paul also speaks of "the spiritual hosts of wickedness in the heavenly places." Does he mean that these have invaded heaven itself? No, when he here speaks of the heavenly places he means that it is the area which does not belong to this earth. It is in line with his emphasis on the fact that these are spiritual forces and therefore do not belong to the mundane. Christians must know the enemy well in order that they may make the proper preparation. He who underestimates the strength of the enemy will be destroyed.

Take the Whole Armor

One is able to speak of the strife of the entire church or of the strife of the individual believer. Paul shows us that the strife is personal and that it is intense as well as a strife of the entire body of believers. Therefore they are to take up the whole armor of God. Every piece has its purpose and the one who will fight in this battle will not be able to do without any part of this armor. Wherever there is a "chink" in the armor, the evil one will find a way to defeat the one who has been careless. But, if the whole armor is employed, you will be able to withstand in the evil day. In other words, victory is guaranteed to those who are faithful and obedient. That evil day of which Paul speaks cannot be avoided. There comes the time in the life of every child of God when he is vulnerable. The evil one then attacks with all his fury. But, even in that evil day you will be able to stand if you are clad with the whole armor of God.

An Offensive Weapon

Although these words are introductory to the description of the various pieces of this whole armor of God and each piece of it does not pass in review here, we must not lose sight of the fact that this armor is not only for defense. It includes also the sword of the Spirit with which the believer goes on the offensive. Jesus told His disciples to go out into the whole world and conquer it for Him by making disciples of all nations. So the church goes out with the gospel throughout the history of the church. So also does the individual believer go out with the claims of Jesus Christ into every area of life. It is true that the believer must be safeguarded in his strife with evil, but more is necessary. He must put on the whole armor of God to do the work of Jesus Christ in this world.

Assured Victory

It is not mere repetition of words when the Apostle says in the closing words of verse 13: "and having done all, to stand." He emphasizes the fact that readers will be able to hold their ground when they have put on the whole armor of God. When all is said and done they will be victorious! The evil one, even with all his power and deceit, has not been able to conquer them. They are then still strong in the Lord and in the strength of His might.

The warning in these words is, of course, clear. The man who is writing these words is indeed inspired by the Spirit of God, but is also writing out of his own experience. How the devil has sought to capture Paul! It seemed as though he had him in his early years, but the Lord took him out of Satan's grasp. Later he fought the good fight — and he kept the faith! No one shall separate us from the love of God! None shall snatch us out of His hand! Strife? Yes, but there is no doubt about the outcome for those who have put on the whole armor of God.

Questions for discussion:
1. Seeing Christ has fought the battle for us, why must we fight for our faith?
2. Is "Knowing the Lord" the same as being strong in the Lord? How do we become strong in the Lord?
3. To believe there is a personal devil is ridiculed today. Do you think the devil appreciates this?
4. How do the ungodly philosophies disturb the faith today? Do you think that the "newer" interpretation of the Bible is included in the present "darkness"?
5. Do we fight valiantly the battle for the truth when we ignore or criticize our confessions? Why?

Lesson 16

The Whole Armor of God

Ephesians 6:14-24

Before coming to the close of this beautiful epistle, Paul goes into detail concerning the armor of God to which he has referred in the previous verses. The interpreter must always be careful that he does justice to the figure which the writer employs, and yet not press every detail concerning the various pieces of armor so that he misses the purpose for which the illustration is used.

An Armed Stand

Paul again begins with the words "stand therefore." This he emphasized in verse 11, "that ye may be able to stand;" verse 13 "that ye may be able to withstand ...and having done all, to stand." There is great danger lurking everywhere for these Ephesian Christians and Paul wants to safeguard them against all the pitfalls of spiritual life. The only way they will be able to hold their ground is by putting on the whole armor of God.

Paul uses the imagery of the armor elsewhere in his writings. In I Thess. 5:8 he mentions some of the pieces of this armor. However, nowhere else does he speak of this armor as completely as he does in this last chapter of Ephesians. He, no doubt, has in mind the Roman soldier of his day. The Roman soldier was well equipped and certainly had been successful. To be able to stand in the spiritual conflict one must be just as well equipped.

The Girdle of Truth

First of all he speaks of the loins being girded with the

truth. He refers to the belt worn by the Roman soldier wherewith he gathered up his loose garments. This is the only way the soldier will be prepared to fight. The Christian must first of all be truthful, sincere, dependable. If he is not, none of the other pieces of armor will do him any good.

The Breastplate of Righteousness

The Roman soldier also had a breastplate which covered the front and back of the person and protected his vital organs. It covered him from the neck to the thighs. This was a most important piece of equipment because it gave protection in battle against both arrow and sword and javelin. The Christian must have a breastplate when he goes into spiritual battle and his breastplate is his righteousness. The righteousness of Christ is not meant, but his own subjective righteousness as a believer. His moral rectitude! No one can do battle, much less stand in that warfare, if his own righteousness is lacking. The life which he lives in obedience to the law of his God must furnish him protection in battle! How can he fight if he does not live the life which is required by his Lord?

The Footwear of the Gospel

The feet must be shod with the preparation of the gospel of peace. The Romans had placed great emphasis on the sturdy footwear of their soldiers because only the well-shod army is able to move quickly and for long distances. The soldier must not be shod with the sandal common to Jewish life. The soldier in the spiritual battle must be ready at any time to move against the opponent. The shoes do not picture the gospel itself, but the preparation to use the gospel! To "buy up the opportunity." To be ready when the opportunity presents itself to bear witness to the gospel of Jesus Christ.

The Shield of Faith

The believer is also commanded to take up the shield of faith wherewith he may be able to quench all the fiery darts of the evil one. The opponents would dip their arrows in a tar-like substance, light them, and then shoot at the opposing army. The shield which the Roman soldier carried was to be used to defend against these arrows. If one would get beyond the shield, great damage would be done and life would be threatened. To say that the Christian warrior must go out in faith is saying the obvious. But, what does this faith accomplish? It is your shield, says the Apostle. Only with that faith will you be able to extinguish the fiery darts which the evil one, the devil, sends at you! Without faith no one will be able to stand. Notice, however, that even when that faith is exercised it does not mean that the evil one will not fire his arrows at the Christian; it only means that these arrows will not penetrate to do vital damage to his person.

The Helmet of Salvation

"And take the helmet of salvation." Who would go into battle with his head uncovered? Such a person would be courting disaster. The soldier of Paul's day placed a sturdy helmet on his head to protect that vital part of the body. Salvation plays that role in the battle of faith, says the Apostle. It is offered! Who would be so foolish that he would not take it? If his salvation is still questionable, a person will soon fall in battle with the evil one. This writer also believes that this salvation protects his *thinking*. Having salvation through the blood of Christ, he will not fall victim to the false philosophies of the world.

The Sword of the Spirit — the Word of God

The Christian must also take the sword of the Spirit, which is the word of God. This is really the only offensive weapon mentioned. There are some commentators who see offensive properties in some of the other parts of this armor, but this seems farfetched. However, the sword is the primary weapon of offense. No soldier is merely going to stand on the battlefield well-protected against all opposing weapons; he is there first of all to conquer! The only offensive weapon of the Christian, says Paul, is the word of God! But, remember, *that* is the sword of the Spirit. It is Spirit filled and directed. With that sword one is able to vanquish any foe. Let the Christian realize that with this sword he invades the territory of the opposition and conquers the opposition. The child of God is not standing, though well protected, on a battlefield to see whether or not he will be able to endure. No, he must go on the attack! That sword has wrought great things! If that sword is blunted in any way, the Christian is helpless. The imagery used by the apostle in this chapter should alert us to the dangers whereby we are surrounded. It is not only Satan's arrows which we are to fear; we are to fear the attempts to take the sword of the Spirit out of our hands!

Completely Equipped

Equipped with this whole armor of God (panoply), the believer will be able to stand. He is not placed as a defenseless individual in the midst of this world. The Lord does not throw him to the wolves! God gives him whatever he needs to be able not only to stand, but even to rob Satan of his ill-gotten goods. The Christian is not able to get along with less than that which is here offered. He must take up the whole armor of God!

Indispensable Prayer

The whole armor of God reveals to us how much the believer has received out of the hand of his God to be able to function in the way he should in this world. Many indeed are the spiritual gifts given to the child of God.

Properly using these he will be able to stand in the evil day. However, there is one other item absolutely necessary in order that he may be able to stand. This is prayer. He cannot live without it.

He must even put on each part of the armor prayerfully. This is also the, way he goes into battle — with prayer and supplication. He prays on all occasions and he does so in harmony with the Spirit of God. Such a person perseveres in prayer for all the saints. He lives in the spirit of the communion of saints. Prayers one for another are natural to those who love the Lord.

Paul also asks that the readers may remember him in their prayers. We must remember that he was in prison at the time he wrote this epistle. This was the first imprisonment at Rome. He does not ask them to pray for his release, but that "utterance may be given unto me." He prays that he will be found faithful in the infrequent occasions he has to bear testimony to his Lord. Of course, he is not able to go out to preach the gospel as in former days. But, he is in the presence of members of the Roman guard. He may also be brought into a courtroom again. Let him then be able to give the word of God to those who are his jailors. Boldness in making known the mystery of the gospel will be difficult. May he have the spiritual strength in that day to be faithful!

Ambassador in Chains

The fact that he is in prison is not one which he seeks to hide as though he is ashamed of it, because he is being held in prison on account of his faithfulness. Those who are not faithful to their Lord are not being imprisoned by Caesar. It is a badge of honor that he is in prison. But, he is an "ambassador" in prison. He is the emissary of the great King. Surely, the King whom he represents will not allow him to remain in prison! Let those who have incarcerated him realize that they are hereby bringing dishonor on the name of the King whom Paul represents. We would also think that this man ought to be free to publish abroad the gospel of Jesus Christ. But no, his Lord allows him to be imprisoned so that he may speak to an individual here and another later and that he may have time to write these glorious prison epistles!

Faithful Helpers

There has been concern in the churches about the Apostle's welfare. The very fact that they receive an epistle from his hand cheers them but they would like to know more of the details concerning his life. Tychicus is bringing this letter. He is a most dependable helper of Paul. When he comes they will be able to ask Tychicus and he will be able to tell them how Paul is doing. What a blessing that this man has helpers whom he can trust. He can trust them with the precious letters which have been laboriously written and can also trust them to comfort the hearts of the members of the churches. Timothy and Titus; are such helpers, as is also Tychicus. Paul always has the welfare of the churches in mind. He is afraid that the people may fall away from the way which he has shown them. They must be helped. They must not draw the wrong conclusions from the fact that he is imprisoned. Let them put on the whole armor of God prayerfully, and let them remember him in these prayers.

Benediction

A beautiful benediction closes the book. He speaks of peace and love and faith and grace to be given to them by God the Father and the Lord Jesus Christ. Many have wondered about the order in which these blessings are named. This is a totally useless exercise. All these blessings belong to the brethren. All these proceed only from the Triune God. The Apostle ends with a beautiful description of the "brethren." They are those who love the Lord Jesus

Christ with an imperishable love.

In the communion of saints; in the body of Jesus Christ; in the church of our Blessed Redeemer are all the blessings found of which he has spoken in this letter. It is a wonderful benefit to belong to the true church of Christ!

Questions for discussion:

1. How are the details of an illustration sometimes pressed so that we lose sight of the meaning the author has in mind? Is this also done with the interpretation of parables?

2. In I Thess. 5:8 the same author speaks of "the breastplate of faith and love," while here he speaks of the "breastplate of righteousness." Is there a conflict? Must these passages be harmonized? Or could you imagine that this "breastplate" might even mean other things in other connections?

3. Is the "sword of the Spirit which is the word of God" still quite sharp today? Do those who deny the factual character of any part of Scripture still have the "sword of the Spirit"?

4. Can anything be accomplished, even in full armor, without prayer?

5. Would any king worthy of the name, allow his ambassador to another land to be imprisoned? Do God's ways sometimes shake our faith?

6. Why is Ephesians an important part of Scripture?

Notes

Notes

Notes

Notes

Notes